Learning and Change
in the Adult Years

Mark Tennant
Philip Pogson

Learning and Change in the Adult Years

A Developmental Perspective

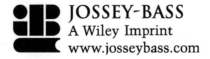

JOSSEY-BASS
A Wiley Imprint
www.josseybass.com

Published by Jossey-Bass
A Wiley Imprint
989 Market Street, San Francisco, CA 94103-1741 www.josseybass.com

Jossey-Bass books and products are available through most bookstores. To contact Jossey-Bass directly call our Customer Care Department within the U.S. at 800-956-7739, outside the U.S. at 317-572-3986 or fax 317-572-4002.

Jossey-Bass also publishes its books in a variety of electronic formats. Some content that appears in print may not be available in electronic books.

Excerpt from "Animula Vagula Blandula" from *Memoirs of Hadrian* by Marguerite Yourcenar and translated by Grace Fricke. Copyright © 1959, reprinted by permission of Martin Secker & Warburg, Ltd. Copyright © 1963 by Marguerite Yourcenar. Copyright renewed © 1991 by Yannick Gillou. Reprinted by permission of Farrar, Straus & Giroux, Inc.

The list from DeCorte, 1990, in Chapter Six is reprinted from *European Journal of Psychology Education*, 1990, Vol. 5, pp. 5–19, with permission from Elsevier Science Ltd., Pergamon Imprint, The Boulevard, Langford Lane, Kidlington OX5 1GB, UK.

Library of Congress Cataloging-in-Publication Data

Tennant, Mark.
   Learning and change in the adult years : a developmental perspective / Mark Tennant and Philip Pogson. — 1st ed.
       p.   cm. — (Jossey-Bass higher and adult education series) (Social and behavioral science series)
   Includes bibliographical references and index.
   ISBN 0-7879-0082-6 (alk. paper)
   ISBN 0-7879-6498-0 (paperback)
   1. Adulthood—Psychological aspects.   2. Learning, Psychology of.
3. Adult learning.   I. Pogson, Philip.   II. Title.   III. Series: Jossey-Bass higher and adult education series.   IV. Series: Jossey-Bass social and behavioral science series.
BF724.5.T46   1995
155.6—dc20   94-42160

FIRST EDITION
HB Printing   10 9 8 7 6 5 4 3
PB Printing   10 9 8 7 6 5 4 3 2

A *joint publication in*

The Jossey-Bass

Higher and Adult Education Series

and

The Jossey-Bass

Social and Behavioral Science Series

Consulting Editor
Adult and Continuing Education

Alan B. Knox
University of Wisconsin, Madison

Contents

Preface

This book explores the significance of the psychological literature on adult development for an understanding of adult education issues and practices. In particular, it focuses on the implications of the developmental literature for three core areas of concern in adult education: how to acknowledge the experience of learners, how to promote autonomy and self-direction, and how to establish an "adult" teacher-learner relationship. It thus offers a developmental perspective on how to approach and understand adult teaching and learning.

Scope and Purpose

Learning and Change in the Adult Years differs from other treatments of this topic in that it investigates the developmental literature from the point of view of some core concerns facing adult educators: about experience and how it generates developmental change; about the changing relationship between self and other across the life span (and the implications for the teacher-learner relationship); and about the processes that promote psychological qualities such as separateness, independence, interdependence, and autonomy. To expand on this last concern a little: many adult educators seek to promote learner autonomy, using a variety of techniques. Adopting a developmental perspective would mean reexamining these techniques in the light of the developmental literature: How does learner autonomy relate to being an autonomous person more generally? Is autonomy a developmental imperative? What, if anything, precedes autonomy as a psychological construct?

Ultimately, the aim of the book is to assist adult educators (or, more broadly, those who have any sort of educational role) to understand their practice from a developmental perspective. In most cases, this will mean posing new questions and discovering new issues, thereby enhancing educators' capacity to analyze and improve practice. It also offers a new way of incorporating the developmental literature into the adult education literature. The developmental literature should not be seen as providing a foundation of knowledge that is then applied to adult education. Instead, the two areas should be seen as having different approaches to common concerns and interests, which if integrated can enhance the understanding of adulthood and adult learning and education.

Our interest in writing this book stems from a conviction that adult education and adult development are inextricably bound. There has always been an acknowledgment of the relevance of adult development in the adult education literature, but the question posed has been, How can the findings be used to improve my teaching and program planning? rather than, How can an understanding of the issues and dilemmas of adult development inform my practice as an adult educator? The former question demands that the literature provide reasonably unambiguous principles or models to help us plan, conduct, and evaluate learning. When the literature fails in this, the temptation is to dismiss it as irrelevant (see, for example, Courtenay, 1994). The latter question allows for competing views and a higher level of uncertainty or ambiguity in the literature and implies that one's practice as an educator can benefit from engagement in debate on issues relating to adult development. This is the point of view we adopt in the book. Moreover, we believe that many of the larger questions regarding adult development (such as, Toward what end should development tend?) require judgments of value, and therefore in principle are not resolvable in any scientific sense. Finally, one can discern implicit views of adult development in the everyday practice of adult educators: in the way they relate to students, analyze their learning difficulties, or dissect their motives and personal characteristics. By engaging in the process of promoting adult learning, adult educators inevitably become engaged with adult development. The better they understand the issues, the more effective their work will be.

Overview of the Contents

Following an introductory chapter, the book is conceptually divided into three parts: two chapters on the development of thought and knowledge, two chapters on the development of the self, and four chapters on the relationship between adult development and adult education practice. The introductory chapter, Chapter One, foreshadows the themes and directions of the book. Chapter Two begins by reviewing the performance of adults on standard intelligence tests. After a critique of these tests, the chapter explores the distinctly adult qualities of intelligence. The argument is that adult intellectual and cognitive growth is predicated on the experience of dealing with everyday problems at work or at home and that our concept of adult intelligence needs to recognize this. Chapter Three documents the literature on practical intelligence, tacit knowledge, and expertise. These are all portrayed as developmental phenomena dependent on the experience of dealing with everyday problems and tasks. Given that much of adult education is directed toward enhancing the student's ability to deal with such problems and tasks, this branch of the literature has much to offer.

The next two chapters discuss the development of the self. Chapter Four reviews theories of the life course, exploring the themes of the relationship between self and other over the life span, the role of experience in development, and the importance of autonomy as a developmental concept. Chapter Four concludes by asking, To what extent do social and cultural groupings construct and then prescribe the life course patterns of their members? Chapter Five addresses this question by outlining the ways in which social and historical influences shape the life course and the presence of these influences in adult education theories and practices, especially those aimed at promoting individual change and transformation.

The remaining four chapters focus on the adult education literature, but from a developmental perspective, making reference to the preceding material. Chapter Six examines the nature of personal autonomy, its status as a developmental phenomenon, educational strategies used to promote it, and its limits within a given social context. Chapter Seven looks at the various ways in which adult educators have attempted to incorporate experiences into learning and the way in which the self interprets and endows experience with meaning. Chapter Eight explores the political and psychological dimensions of the teaching role and the need for a teacher to develop an identity or posture. The final chapter poses the question, What does it mean to have a developmental perspective on teaching? It serves as a summary of the main themes and arguments.

Audience

The book is primarily aimed at adult education practitioners, preferably with some background in psychology, who are engaged in formal study at master's or doctoral level. However, *Learning and Change in the Adult Years* is accessible also to practitioners who have not formally studied either psychology or adult education. Anyone whose work requires some thought about how adults learn and develop will find that we address familiar concerns.

The writing of the book commenced in November 1992, while the principal author was staying at West Hampstead in the home so generously made available by Nod Miller and her partner. Many of the chapters are based on previously published articles. A portion of Chapter Three appeared in *New Education* (Tennant, 1991c), Chapter Five is based on an article in *Adult Education Quarterly* (Tennant, 1993), and much of Chapter Six appeared in the *Australian Journal of Adult Education* (Tennant, 1991b).

We wish to acknowledge our respective partners for their contribution to this work, our colleagues at the University of Technology, Sydney, for providing such a stimulating environment in which

to work, and our academic adult education colleagues, who collectively contribute to a better understanding of this important, interesting, and exciting field.

Sydney, Australia   Mark Tennant
February 1995   Philip Pogson

The Authors

Mark Tennant is dean of the University Graduate School at the University of Technology, Sydney. He has published numerous articles in international journals on the theme of life-span development and learning. His book *Psychology and Adult Learning* (1988) won the 1990 Cyril O. Houle Award for outstanding literature in adult education. Tennant obtained his Ph.D. degree (1983) in psychology from Macquarie University.

Philip Pogson is director of "The Leading Partnership," a consulting firm specializing in strategic management and business development based in Sydney, Australia. He has held senior human resources and organizational development roles in the private and public sectors and in vocational training for people who are disadvantaged and unemployed long-term. Pogson completed his master's degree (1994) in adult education at the University of Technology, Sydney.

Learning and Change
in the Adult Years

Chapter One

Relationships Between Development and Learning in Adulthood

Adulthood is a time of development and change, but its processes differ from those of childhood. Much of the identity of adult education is based on the distinctive qualities of the adult learner as opposed to the child learner. Thus questions about the distinctive qualities of adults are a natural and necessary part of the profession of adult education.

Adult education is a developmental enterprise, but what do adult educators need to understand about development? We argue that there are three broad areas of development that need to be addressed by adult educators: the development of adult learning capacity, the investment of the "self" in learning, and the link between social development and personal development.

The Development of Adult Learning Capacity

What assumptions about adult learning capacities do we bring to the adult classroom? Are conventional notions of intelligence useful in understanding adults' capacities? Is there a distinct quality to their intelligence? If so, how do we as educators acknowledge these qualities in program planning, curriculum design, teaching techniques, materials development, assessment, and so on?

It is customary to distinguish between two domains of theory and research in adult development: the development of intellectual or cognitive functioning, and the development of personality and social roles. The former has received somewhat less attention in the adult education literature than the latter. The reason for this is

1

uncertain. Perhaps it is because the very idea of measuring and grading intellectual capacity does not sit well with the egalitarian ethos of adult education. Adult educators have been more comfortable with the notions of cognitive or learning styles, which describe learners as being "different" rather than "superior" or "inferior" on some quantitative scale. Also, the early findings in the domain of intellectual and cognitive development were not particularly heartening for adult educators. Initially, two models prevailed. One, the *stability model*, assumed that adult cognition remained essentially the same after maturity. In this view, once a growing child's cognitive progress achieved mature forms of reasoning and thinking, there was no significant change throughout the adult years. By contrast, the *decrement model* postulated a gradual decrease in the adult individual's capacity to utilize and organize information, presumably the result of some kind of biological deterioration. Contemporary theory and research rejects both these models, replacing them with a model of intellectual and cognitive growth during the adult years. This growth is based on the experience of dealing with concrete problems and situations at work, in the home, and in community life. It often fails to show up on intelligence tests. These tests have long been recognized as culture-specific, but there is an emerging view that conventional tests are also *age-specific*, that is, they employ problems and tasks familiar to schoolchildren but rarely seen by adults. Researchers have begun to recommend that intelligence tests for adult populations draw on the kinds of problems and situations that are found in adult life.

A similar argument has been advanced by those who have sought to extend the Piagetian view of cognitive development to the adult years. The view that formal operational thought develops in early adolescence and is then applied throughout the adult years has been challenged by Riegel (1973), Labouvie-Vief (1980a, b, and c, 1985), Basseches (1984), and Rybash, Hoyer, and Roodin (1986). They point to the characteristic quality of real-life problems as opposed to the logical, physical, or mathematical problem-solving exercises devised by Piaget. Real-life problems are said to be open ended rather than closed, that is, although they have no single correct and logical solution, they require a person to commit to a single course of action: buy one home, send a child to one school, begin one new job out of all the possibilities life offers.

The general argument being pursued in the literature, then, is that the formal (logical) properties of a task or problem become less important during the adult years. This is because adult intellectual and cognitive growth centers on the accumulation of experience in dealing with the concrete problems adults encounter. For this reason, the particular content of a problem and the context in which it is set become increasingly important with age. Chapter Two explores the literature on intelligence testing.

This search for a distinctly adult quality to intelligence and cognition has inspired some more recent work on practical intelligence (Sternberg and Wagner, 1986), wisdom (Sternberg, 1990a), and the development of expertise (Chi, Glaser, and Farr, 1988), work that reinforces the significance of experience as the locus of developmental growth in adulthood. Concepts such as practical intelligence, wisdom, and expertise, however, introduce a new dimension to our understanding of why it is that experience is so central a concept in adult teaching and learning. And it may well be that this emerging literature will help shape our thinking about how best to utilize experience for learning. Chapter Three examines the literature on the role of experience.

The Investment of the "Self" in Learning

Adult education is certainly a site for self-development, either explicitly or implicitly. Given that there is considerable investment of the self in any learning situation, the learning experience can have an impact on learners' self-concept or self-esteem, or even their sense of identity. How does the sense of self and identity change over the adult years and what are the educational implications? In particular, what are the implications for adult education programs targeted toward life-cycle issues?

The development of personality and social roles (the self) occupies a wide spectrum of psychological literature on developmental stages, the life cycle, and the phases of adult life. Works range from essentially descriptive accounts of age-related social behavior (Havighurst, 1972; Levinson, 1978; Gould, 1978) to the various attempts to identify the stages and processes of the development of self, ego, or personality (Erikson, 1959; Loevinger, 1976). This domain seems to have had the greater influence in shaping views about adult teaching and learning. For example, it is said that much of the impetus for adult learning emerges from the developmental tasks or concerns associated with different phases of the life cycle (McCoy, 1977; Knox, 1979; Weathersby, 1981; Cross, 1981). Also, the various conceptions of personality development provide for adult educators a raison d'être: the stimulation and promotion of personal growth and development.

The idea that one's personality or identity changes and/or develops during the adult years is now generally accepted. Furthermore, the different theoretical approaches all take a position on the relationship between experience and development, the role of autonomy as a developmental construct, and the emergence of notions of self and other throughout the life cycle. Chapter Four discusses these ideas.

The development of personality and social roles has also been viewed as having its origins in social practices rather than innate psychological processes. Some argue that the self is at least partly socially constituted, while others go further and argue that the very concept of self-development over the life course, with its putative phases and stages of development, is itself a social construct. This compounds the problem of how social forces act to constrain the ability of the self to interpret experience. Not only is experience channelled through a social filter, but the social filter itself changes and develops throughout the life course in a largely predictable fashion as individuals come to live out the age-graded expectations placed upon them at different phases of life. Chapter Five discusses the emerging theories of "life course" as a social construct.

The Link Between Social Development
and Personal Development

A key argument in this book is that adult development can only have meaning in a given social and historical context. By and large, development is said to occur when we observe growth in those qualities which we as a society value: whether it be the capacity to think of alternative solutions to problems, to group unlike objects in creative new ways, to be more autonomous, to resolve childhood conflicts and anxieties, or to be intimate without a loss of personal identity. Because values are contested in any pluralist society, it follows that the meaning of development is also contested. Thus development is not solely a psychological construct, it is also a social construct—and different versions of what it means to be "developed" serve the interests of different groups. The implication for adult education practice is that educators must adopt a critical stance in relation to claims about development so that the alternative views of development can be recognized.

The various forms of adult education provision are driven by both the circumstances of adulthood and the prevailing social and economic conditions. Thus self-development is not simply a matter of the perfectibility of the person (see Houle, 1992, p. 227), it also includes the capacity to resist prevailing social and economic conditions which potentially lead to alienation and enslavement. Second, educational opportunities need to respond to life-cycle patterns that are changing as a result of demographic changes and changes in the sexual division of labor, the nature of the workplace, the length of working life, the length of a working day, and so on. Education can foster diversity and choice and complement the increased diversity of life-cycle patterns. Third, the obsolescence of knowledge and skills during working life is a powerful force for distributing learning opportunities across the life span, and learning is now firmly entrenched as a key element of every stage and phase of life. Finally, learning and personal development are predicated on a measure of democracy and equality—learning can only proceed effectively when there is an absence of external constraint.

More recently, Knox (1993) makes the point that adult education provision typically responds to both social and personal concerns. His summary of media reports on adult education programs in the United States provides a nice illustration of the range of adult education activities, and how they contain both a social and a personal development dimension. He finds the following examples (pp. 4–5):

University—U.S. universities adapt videotapes from engineering and management courses for part-time students; the tapes are to be used by universities in Central and Eastern Europe and the former Soviet Union to help engineers and managers there adapt to market economies.

Literacy—Two university departments assist various community agencies engaged in adult basic education by providing staff development activities for paid staff, community volunteers, and university students who tutor and assist functionally illiterate adults to improve their reading, writing, and math.

Minorities—A community college, community agency, and several religious institutions cooperate in offering educational activities such as English as a foreign language and vocational education for refugee families from several countries and subcultures that must make similar adjustments.

Distance—A public broadcasting station announces several new program series and study guides that provide opportunities for adults who might otherwise be deterred by location or other commitments.

Workplace—An enterprise expands its retraining and staff development activities to increase economic productivity and quality improvement.

Corrections—A correctional education program at a state prison is reduced because of overcrowding, combined with cuts in state funding that formerly allowed a local community college to provide instructors for adult education courses in the prison.

Family—A social worker works intensively for months on educational activities for an entire family to reduce dysfunctionality as an alternative to placing the children in foster homes.

Professions—A professional association conducts a workshop for members on new knowledge, implications for professional practice, and benefits for clients.

Elders—A private organization announces upcoming domestic and international study tours for increasing numbers of better educated and affluent older adults who seldom attend activities at local senior citizens centers.

Rural—The Cooperative Extension Service offers a wide variety of educational programs and services in a rural county on agricultural production, conservation, family life, nutrition, leadership of youth groups, and community problem solving.

Health—Major features of Alcoholics Anonymous's twelve-step program, such as individual responsibility and peer support, are adapted to other self-help groups concerned with drug dependency, weight loss, smoking cessation, and various health conditions.

Community—Community groups and government agencies collaborate on a series of nonformal educational sessions to explore causes and possible solutions following violence in a poor neighborhood.

These activities have their origin in social and historical circumstances: political change, poverty, migration, urbanization, the aging of the population, family disintegration, increasing international competition, and health concerns such as obesity and drug dependence. Ultimately, however, these phenomena impact upon the life concerns of individuals: the struggle to learn a new language, to read and write, to overcome drug addiction, to maintain health, to increase work-related skills, and to participate in family and community life. These are all intensely personal, and they involve a significant investment of the self.

Adult Development and the Principles of Adult Learning

There have been many attempts to distill the principles of adult teaching and learning. However, the use of the term principle does not seem appropriately applied to adult teaching and learning on a number of counts. First, "principle" is surely too strong a term to apply to teaching and learning. It may be appropriate in fields such as science, where cause/effect relationships can be identified in experimental laboratories, or where all known variables can be controlled or randomized, or where the principle in question is universal or a priori, and not subject to social, historical, or cultural variation. But teaching is a human pursuit where variables are not controlled, where outcomes are not predictable, where individual and group variations appear to swamp any universal lawlike features, and where the perceptions and expectations of the moment can in themselves affect the outcome of any intervention. In this scenario, it is simply not possible to apply a "principles-to-practice" formula like that implied in the term principle.

Second, although the term principle can be used in the normative sense of being something that can be invoked to guide one's practice, there are many circumstances where principles come into conflict. Indeed, practice is more likely to produce tensions between opposing principles than harmony between like principles. Third, principles are open to interpretation, and it can be difficult to be certain whether a particular action exemplifies or transgresses a given principle.

Finally, the very use of the term principle contains assumptions about adult teaching and learning, namely that the teacher is privileged in relation to the learner, so that it is the teacher who "knows" the principles of teaching as certainly as he or she "knows" the subject matter, and the learners become the passive objects to which the principles are applied. In the worst case, learners who question certain teaching practices will be silenced by invoking the principles. Principles can thus be used to stifle rather than create debate, and to domesticate rather than empower learners.

Teaching is above all an interactive process: learners interacting with teachers, learners interacting with other learners, learners interacting with the material being investigated or produced, and both learners and teachers in continuing interaction with the social and psychological forces around them. Rather than using a set of static principles to understand these interactions, this book seeks to identify the tensions inherent within them. One way of approaching this task is to take the "principles" of adult learning, at least in the way they have been presented in the adult education literature over the last thirty years, and recast them so they express a number of fundamental concerns to be addressed in each new teaching situation. Thus there is a concern with

Acknowledging the experience of learners

Establishing an adult teacher-learner relationship

Promoting autonomy and self-direction

Each of these concerns contains a tension or set of tensions that are dynamic rather than static and that arguably reveal more about the practice of adult teaching and learning than hitherto revealed from a principles-to-practice approach. Moreover, the developmental literature has something to say about each of these tensions, as we hope to illustrate in Chapters Six, Seven, and Eight.

Conclusion

Although this book emphasizes the unique features of adulthood and the special characteristics of adults as learners and adult education as a field of practice, it is important not to lose sight of the notions of adult development and lifelong learning and education. "Learning to Be" is indeed a continuous, lifelong pursuit, one in which the self struggles to preserve continuity with past experiences and, simultaneously, to change and develop in order to make sense of current and future experiences. This ongoing tension between continuity and change lies at the heart of what it means to develop and learn across the life span.

Chapter Two

Intellectual and Cognitive Development During the Adult Years

The relationship between aging and intelligence is crucial for an understanding of adult learning. If there are systematic changes in intellectual functioning with age, then adult educators need to understand and respond to these changes. Does general intelligence increase, decrease, or remain stable over the life span? Or do some aspects of intelligence increase while others decline? From an educator's point of view, it is important to know the extent of individual differences in any general pattern of growth or decline, the source of changes in intellectual functioning, and whether individual changes can be modified through some kind of intervention. But the relationship between aging and intelligence is problematic, principally because the concept of intelligence itself is so problematic.

This chapter commences with an overview of research that has employed standard intelligence tests to investigate the relationship between intelligence and aging. It then explores the problems and issues involved in using standard tests to measure intelligence, and presents some newly conceived views on what constitutes intellectual capacity during the adult years.

Age and Performance on Standard Intelligence Tests

Early studies of the development of intelligence during adulthood revealed a decline in intellectual capacity with age, which was attributed to loss of brain function. However, the work of Baltes

(1968) and Schaie (1965, 1975) has shown that these early studies, which only measured generational differences in performance, misinterpreted those differences as indicators of developmental change. Such generational differences were due to the increased availability of formal educational opportunities. Intelligence test scores improve with education, and when different generations are tested at the same time (that is, the test sample includes people reflecting a cross-section of ages), generational differences in intelligence test results are confounded with differences in intelligence due to age. Thus the extent of educational opportunity rather than age may explain the decline in intelligence test scores with age. Schaie and his colleagues (Schaie, 1983; Schaie and Hertzog, 1983; Schaie and Willis, 1986) sought to overcome this problem by designing studies that control for age, cohort (year of birth), and time-of-measurement effects (the year the tests were administered). The researchers used a combination of cross-sectional and longitudinal designs: in addition to testing heterogeneous groups, they followed some of the same people and retested them over many years. For example, Schaie (1983) reports on the results of a twenty-one-year study comprising a series of independent cross-sectional studies that used the group-administered Primary Mental Abilities (PMA) test, with groups being measured in 1956, 1963, 1970, and 1977. He conducted a longitudinal investigation, in conjunction with the last three cross-sectional studies. The key finding was that intelligence does decline with chronological age, but the decrease does not begin until relatively late in life. Figure 2.1 shows the results for three PMA subtests—verbal meaning, space, and reasoning—from ages twenty-one to eighty-one. It shows *verbal meaning* increasing until age fifty-three and then declining from sixty-three to seventy-four, *space* peaking at forty-six and also declining rapidly between sixty-seven and seventy-four, and *reasoning* declining after age sixty. It should be emphasized that these results are corrected for biases due to cohort and time of measurement. However, it should also be noted that where decline is found, it can normally be reversed through training (Baltes and Willis, 1982; Schaie and Willis, 1986).

Figure 2.1. Age and Performance on the
Primary Mental Abilities Subtests.

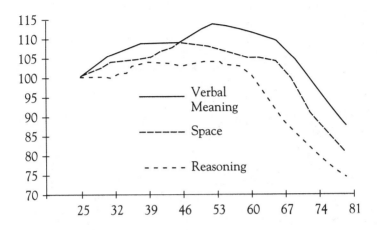

Source: Schaie, 1983; reproduced in Kaufman, 1990, p. 211.

The question of intellectual change across the adult life span has also been addressed using the Wechsler Adult Intelligence Scale (WAIS-R, 1981). The WAIS-R is an individually administered test, widely used for clinical assessment, consisting of a verbal scale and a performance scale. Each scale has a number of subtests, as outlined in Table 2.1.

Figures 2.2, 2.3, and 2.4 show the mean IQs (using the WAIS-R) for a number of age groups from twenty to seventy-four, with and without a control for education. Figure 2.2 graphs full-scale IQ, and Figures 2.3 and 2.4 separate the data for verbal IQ and performance IQ. When corrected for educational opportunity, verbal IQ maintains or increases its level until the sixties and early seventies. In contrast, performance IQ shows a clear decline with age.

The age difference between different components of IQ is consistent with the theory of fluid/crystallized intelligence proposed by Cattell (1971) and Horn (1970, 1982). They separate intellectual abilities into two general clusters, *fluid* and *crystallized* intelligence

Table 2.1. Subtests of the WAIS-R.

Verbal Scale Tasks	Examples
Information	
The knowledge expected of an average person with average opportunities	• Name four presidents of the United States. • Who wrote *Hamlet*?
Digit Span	
The ability to repeat digits in the same or reverse order	• 5–8–2 to 7–1–3–94–2–5–6–8.
Vocabulary	
The ability to explain the meaning of words.	• Explain the meaning of regulate, designate, impale, tangible.
Arithmetic	
The computational skills associated with everyday life	• A person with $18.00 spends $7.90. How much is left? • Eight people finish a job in six days. How many people are needed to finish it in half a day?
Comprehension	
The commonsense understanding of everyday experiences and the ability to explain reasons for actions or the meaning of common expressions	• Why are people who are born deaf usually unable to talk? • What does this saying mean: "Strike while the iron is hot"?
Similarities	

The ability to identify abstract properties linking different objects or ideas	• In what ways are these alike?
	  Orange—Banana
	  Eye—Ear
	  Praise—Punishment

Performance Scale Tasks	Examples
Picture completion	

The ability to identify the missing detail on pictures of familiar subjects	• Picture Missing part
	  Door Knobs
	  Man Finger
	  Boat Oar lock
	  Map Florida

Table 2.1. Subtests of the WAIS-R, Cont'd.

Performance Scale Tasks	Examples
Picture arrangement	

The ability to place a series of pictures in a sequence so they tell a credible story	• Three to six cards that tell a plausible story
	    1. A bird is building a nest.
	    2. The eggs are laid.
	    3. The chicks are hatched.

Block design	
The ability to reproduce a given design from a number of patterned blocks	• Red and white blocks manipulated to copy a design displayed on a card.
Object Assembly	
The ability to place pieces of an object together to form a whole object	• A hand or elephant divided into seven or eight pieces (similar to a typical jigsaw puzzle).
Digit symbol	

The ability to quickly substitute symbols for digits by reproducing the substituted symbol where a digit occurs	• Replace
	    1 with −
	    2 with ∧
	    3 with ´
	    8 with x
	    9 with =

Note: Examples are based on the Wechsler Adult Intelligence Scale, 1955.

(which are similar to Wechsler's performance and verbal scales, respectively). *Fluid intelligence* is measured by tests of complex reasoning, memory, and figural relations—tests measuring the basic information-processing capacity of the person. *Crystallized intelligence* is measured by tests for information storage, verbal comprehension, and numerical reasoning—abilities normally associated with experience and acculturation (that is, abilities that can be learned). Horn and Cattell both report that these two dimensions of intelligence change in different directions during the adult years. Specifically, from the teenage years onward there is a decrease in

Figure 2.2. Full-Scale IQ (WAIS-R) and Age, with and without a Control for Education.

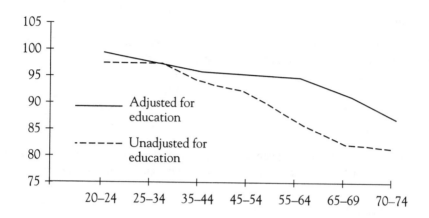

Source: Kaufman, Reynolds, and McLean, 1989. © Ablex Publishing Corp. Reprinted by permission.

fluid intelligence and an increase in crystallized intelligence. The net result is that intellectual functioning remains relatively stable with age, but crystallized intelligence assumes a more prominent role as a component of intellectual functioning. Howard (1988) notes a similar independence in the function of explicit and implicit memory among the aged. That is, in contrast to explicit memory, implicit memory does not diminish with age—although this does not hold true with all tasks in all situations. Howard describes implicit memory as the ability to successfully complete memory tasks that do not require conscious recollection (p. 4).

In summary, research using standard intelligence tests shows some decline in intelligence with age, but not until relatively late in life. In addition, decline, where it is found, can often be reversed through training. Second, those components of intelligence that are based on learning from experience are maintained or even increased over the adult life course. Notwithstanding the plausibility of the results, the intelligence testing tradition has a number of shortcomings that may lead to the devaluation of distinctly adult forms of

Figure 2.3. Verbal IQ (WAIS-R) and Age, with and without a Control for Education.

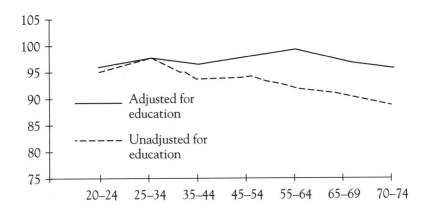

Source: Kaufman, Reynolds, and McLean, 1989. © Ablex Publishing Corp. Reprinted by permission.

intelligence. It is worth exploring this a little further to better understand the reasons for reconceptualizing the intelligence construct so that it adequately reflects these distinctly adult abilities.

Shortcomings in the Standard Tests for Adult Intelligence

Well-documented studies illustrate the shortcomings of using standard tests to measure the intelligence construct outside Western school-based culture. For the purposes of this discussion, there are two important challenges to the validity of intelligence tests. The first asserts that they are too culture-specific; the second, that they are constructed from problems and tasks derived from the context or "culture" of schooling rather than everyday life. Both these challenges derive from a single feature of intelligence tests: that the problems and tasks used are largely decontextualized: that is, separated from everyday social and cultural activities and purposes. The result is that standard tests of intelligence typically

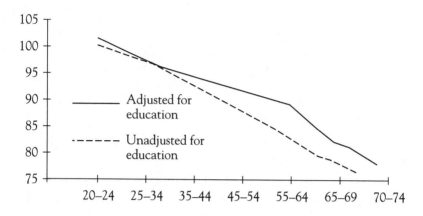

Figure 2.4. Performance IQ (WAIS-R) and Age,
with and without a Control for Education.

Source: Kaufman, Reynolds, and McLean, 1989. © Ablex Publishing Corp. Reprinted by permission.

generate results that undervalue the intellectual capacity of people from non-Western cultures, and of adults whose acquired work and life skills make them less inclined to accept and work within the terms of test problems.

Cultural Specificity of Intelligence Tests

Neisser (1976) cites the work of Cole, Gay, Glick, and Sharp (1971) and Scribner and Cole (1973), who worked with the mostly illiterate and unschooled Kpelle people of Liberia. In the following extract from a conversation between a researcher and a Kpelle man, Neisser cogently exposes the cultural assumptions underlying an attempt to evaluate the thinking skills of the Kpelle, who, "like members of traditional societies everywhere, get poor scores on tests and problems that seem easy to people with some formal education" (pp. 135–136). The following interview protocol illustrates this claim:

Researcher: Flumo and Yakpalo always drink cane juice (rum) together. Flumo is drinking cane juice. Is Yakpalo drinking cane juice?

Subject: Flumo and Yakpalo drink cane juice together, but the time Flumo was drinking the first one, Yakpalo was not there on that day.

Researcher: But I told you that Flumo and Yakpalo always drink cane juice together. One day Flumo was drinking cane juice. Was Yakpalo drinking cane juice that day?

Subject: The day Flumo was drinking the cane juice, Yakpalo was not there on that day.

Researcher: What is the reason?

Subject: The reason is that Yakpalo went to his farm on that day and Flumo remained in town on that day [Neisser 1976, pp. 135–136].

Neisser comments, "Such answers are by no means stupid. The difficulty is that they are not answers *to the questions*." The respondents do not accept the ground rule that is virtually automatic with us: "Base your answer on the terms defined by the questions" (p. 136). Stepping outside the "rules," not accepting them, or simply applying a personal set of rules can result in very poor IQ scores from people unfamiliar with the testing culture—scores that may have no bearing at all on their ability to function in their own context.

In fact, very sophisticated cognitive abilities have been noted among inhabitants of "less developed," non-Western cultures. Gladwin (1970) documented detailed navigational, boat-building, and design abilities among Palowat Atoll natives. Lave (1977a, 1977b) found that Liberian tailors had learned quite high-order mathematical skills without attending formal schools. He found that the generalized cognitive skills of these unschooled tailors derived from their apprenticeship training, where the major learning mode was observation and practice. The verbal instruction and context-free presentations of Western-style schools are not the only possible source of inductive learning.

Dube (1982), Irwin (1991), and others have all found high-level cognitive, memory, and reasoning abilities among non-Western persons who obtained poor results on standard tests featuring abstract and context-free tasks. Carraher, Carraher, and Schliemann (1985) studied street kids in Brazil and found that their subjects could solve mathematical problems embedded in real-life contexts but had difficulty solving school-type word problems and context-free computational problems involving the same numbers and operations. Dube (1982) found high levels of memory and reasoning among both literate and illiterate people in non-Western cultures, and higher levels of memory for story recall among illiterate Africans than among comparable American students.

Informal Test Performance

In a somewhat similar vein in our own culture, researchers have also found that "informal" test performance (that is, performance in applied or everyday situations—what may be referred to as practical intelligence) can be quite different from results achieved in a more prescribed, "formal" environment. For example, in studies made of grocery shoppers in the United States, Murtaugh (1985) followed shoppers through a supermarket, recording their product selections, financial calculations, and other details. Comparisons were made between the accuracy of on-site calculations and the results subjects obtained in subsequent pen-and-paper tests of the same calculations. Scores in the two situations showed substantial differences:

Average correct calculations on tests	59%
Average correct calculations when shopping	98%

Ceci and Bronfenbrenner (1985) found differences in children's performance on a set of tasks in the laboratory as opposed to in home settings. Ceci and Liker (1986) found that the ability of professional punters to predict winning horses was not correlated with IQ as measured by the Wechsler test, despite the very real complexity of the task.

Others have argued that practical intelligence is strongly correlated with the ability to form relationships and social networks. Ford (1982), for example, suggests (as do Walker and Foley, 1973) that social competence represents a domain of human functioning that is at least partly distinguishable from the domain of cognitive or general competence. Goodnow (1986) found that one general feature of practical intelligence is the ability to organize and reorganize plans and thus to go about everyday living efficiently.

Given these findings, it is no wonder that success on an IQ test does not necessarily predict work success. Streufert and Streufert (1978), for example, found little correlation between expertise in business and IQ scores. Ghisselli (1966) and Wigdor and Garner (1982) recorded similar results. Wagner and Sternberg (1986) assert that the typical correlation between occupational performance and employment tests or IQ is about 0.2. Such claims raise serious concerns about the validity of using tests to predict and account for superior workplace performance.

In an interesting historical aside to the issue under consideration, Spearman, an early advocate of IQ testing, wrote the following in a letter to a colleague in 1927 (cited in Miles, 1957, p. 157): "Trabue . . . told of a woman who, although making a bad record in the tests, nevertheless became 'the housekeeper at one of the finest Fifth Avenue hotels, where she successfully directed the work of a corps of approximately fifty maids, three carpenters, two decorators and a plumber.' He was moved to conclude as follows: 'In spite of the evidence of the tests I insist that she is intelligent.'"

The situation faced today is much the same: conventional IQ tests do not necessarily predict real-life success. If this is the case, what models are we to use to evaluate persons who make "a bad record in the tests" but succeed, however we define success, in everyday life? On this point, Sternberg (1988a) relates that psychologists are often "implored to make their research 'ecologically valid,'" that is, "relevant to the real world," and that, "ecologically valid research can yield results that are quite different from those that are not as relevant to the real world" (pp. 287–288).

Although the literature cited above does not form a separate body of conceptually related material that can be said to provide a coherent critique of the psychometric tradition, it does serve to reinforce the fundamentally decontextualized nature of IQ testing. It raises serious questions about the full extent and nature of adult cognitive attributes and reveals the paucity of methodologies to capture them.

It is important to note here that even the users of standardized tests agree with Sternberg and recognize the weakness of applying such tests to real-life problem-solving situations. Harrison, Kaufman, Hickman, and Kaufman (1988) surveyed a group of clinical psychologists, asking them to rate the strengths and weaknesses of the intelligence tests they used. The results appear in Table 2.2.

In summarizing the findings, Kaufman reports, "About one-quarter of the respondents felt that new intelligence tests were needed. Interestingly, those who chose to expand on their perceptions consistently cited the need for intelligence tests that assess practical, social, everyday functioning; that deal more effectively with ethnic-cultural issues; and that assess a broader scope of functions" (1990, p. 17).

These findings reflect a growing understanding of the importance of coming to grips with the full context of human functioning. The complexity of everyday work and home life makes increasing demands on ordinary individuals to negotiate an ever-broadening terrain of life experiences. In the face of such complexity, the narrow focus and circumscribed test regimes of the traditional intelligence tests appear somewhat inadequate for the task.

Table 2.2. Perceived Strong and Weak Attributes of Commonly Used Intelligence Tests for Adolescents and Adults.

Attribute	% Rating Attribute a Strength	% Rating Attribute a Weakness	Difference in Percent
1. Representative standardized sample	67.1	7.4	59.7
2. Development based on sound theoretical principles	62.2	12.4	49.8
3. Guidance in how to interpret the results	47.3	18.7	28.6
4. Relevant content for adults	36.7	15.9	20.8
5. Interest to adults	32.9	18.0	14.9
6. Guidance in how to make meaningful recommendation based on test results	35.7	22.3	13.4
7. Interpreted in the context of lifespan developmental psychology	21.2	35.7	–14.5
8. Measurement of mature decision-making capacities	21.9	37.1	–15.2
9. Relationship to vocational interest and career choice	14.8	40.6	–25.8
10. Real-life problem-solving situations	17.0	43.8	–26.8

Note: Data are based on 283 respondents asked to "rate the following attributes of the intelligence tests you most frequently use for adolescents and adults on a continuum from 1 (significant weakness) to 5 (significant strength)." In this table, "strength" corresponds to ratings of 4 or 5, and "weakness" to ratings of 1 or 2.

Source: Kaufman, 1990, p. 17.

Contemporary Views on the Nature of Adult Intelligence and Cognition

Clearly, the cultural bias of most IQ tests and the very real variations in performance between informal and formal testing militate against their use in real-world environments. There is a need, then, to distinguish between intelligence as an abstract, context-free capacity, and intelligence as the application of capacity in everyday life. Baltes and his co-workers (Baltes, Dittman-Kohli, and Dixon, 1984; Dixon and Baltes, 1986) acknowledge this by distinguishing between the "mechanics" and the "pragmatics" of intelligence. The phrase *mechanics of intelligence* refers to the way a person processes information and solves problems at a basic cognitive level, including the perception of relationships, the formation of classifications, and the extraction of logical conclusions. *Pragmatics of intelligence* refers to the application of the mechanics of intelligence to particular contexts or fields of knowledge. Subsumed under the pragmatics of intelligence are generalized systems of knowledge (also called "crystallized intelligence"); specialized knowledge, such as occupational expertise; and knowledge about the intellectual skills relevant to particular contexts (such as judgments about problem-solving strategies). Baltes and his co-workers argue that the growth of the mechanics of intelligence is confined to childhood and adolescence. If anything, adulthood requires gradual adjustment to losses in this domain. By contrast, the adult years generally bring continuing growth in the "pragmatics" of intelligence.

There is thus emerging a recognition of the need to base intelligence tests for adult populations on the kinds of problems and situations that are pertinent in adult life:

> It is reasonable to assume that the mastering of adult life tasks . . . involves intellectual competencies as well. However, it is also likely that their mastery extends beyond the use of basic cognitive skills as required in formal logic and beyond that knowledge dependent primarily on school-related content. This is certainly true for real life accomplishments associated with careers and career settings . . . in contrast to the assessment of both child and adult intelligence, it is likely that criteria for success in the adult tasks described do not involve primarily a single criterion of logical truth (or accuracy). Rather, application of contextual knowledge systems and of multiple criteria of efficacy may be involved [Baltes, Dittman-Kohli, and Dixon, 1984, p. 50].

This assessment is consistent with recent formulations on the nature of intelligence, such as Sternberg's triarchic theory of intelligence (1984a, 1984b). The first of the three subtheories in the triarchic theory is labeled the "contextual subtheory." In this subtheory, intelligent behavior is defined in large part by the sociocultural context in which it takes place. Contextually intelligent behavior involves the ability to adapt to the environment, select a better environment, or shape the given environment so that it affords a better fit with one's skills, interests, and values. This, of course, is very similar to Baltes's concept of "pragmatic intelligence," which he believes to be the centerpiece of intelligence during the adult years.

In summary, within the intelligence-testing tradition there is now an awareness of the multidimensional and multidirectional nature of intellectual development. That is, people are considered to possess a range of mental abilities, which grow and change in different ways. This conception opens the way for identifying the new forms of intelligence that emerge during adulthood and old age.

The Cognitive-Structuralist Tradition

Recent commentary in the cognitive-structuralist tradition shares the emphasis on the pragmatics of intelligence as an aspect of intellectual growth during the adult years. The conventional view is presented by Piaget and Inhelder (1969). In their description of cognitive development, they postulate a number of stages through which everyone progresses in an invariant sequence. These stages represent qualitatively different ways of making sense, understanding, and constructing a knowledge of the world. Thus children progress through different types of thinking as they develop toward mature adult thought. This process culminates in early adolescence with the attainment of what is termed formal operations, the capacity to think abstractly and reason logically and scientifically, which is applied throughout the adult years. In this view, there is no further development of any major kind beyond formal operations.

Recent commentary, however, highlights the limitations of formal operations as a description of mature adult thought. (See, for example, Alexander and Langer, 1990; Langer and others, 1990; Richards and Commons, 1990; and Irwin, 1991.) The available data on the acquisition of formal operations suggest it is not a single unified capacity operating independently of content and context. Rather, formal thinking skills may be acquired in certain domains and content areas and not in others, depending on the individual's unique aptitudes, interests, motivation, and life experiences.

The later work of Piaget did, it should be noted, take something of this revised view into account. "All normal subjects attain the stage of formal operations or structuring if not between 11–12 to 14–15 years, in any case between 15 and 20 years. However, they reach this stage in different areas according to their aptitudes and their professional specializations (advanced studies or different types of apprenticeship for the various trades)" (Piaget, 1972, pp. 9–10).

This revised position of Piaget is significant because it indicates that he began to appreciate how the reasoning capacity a person brings to bear on a problem may be determined by the context in which the problem is set.

There have been some attempts to extend the cognitive-structuralist tradition and identify further *postformal* stages of cognitive development (Riegel, 1973; Labouvie-Vief, 1980c, 1985; Kramer, 1983; Basseches, 1984; Rybash, Hoyer, and Roodin, 1986). Kohlberg and Ryncarz (1990), for example, postulate the existence of a seventh stage of human development, a *metaphoric* stage, in which "a sense of unity with the cosmos, nature or God is expressed in such a way as to resolve . . . ultimate questions" (p. 191). Souvaine (1990) agrees that the formal operations stage is not the highest point in human development. The authors argue that being able even to describe formal operations bespeaks Piaget's "ability to stand somewhere 'outside' the system." Finally, Irwin (1991) claims that the concept of formal operations does not allow for the existence of dialectical thought, because it takes as its object "the idealized epistemic subject and not the development of a concrete acting subject situated in a particular moment in time and history" (p. 44).

The general view expressed is that mature adult cognition is characterized by the ability to fit abstract thinking into the concrete limitations of everyday life. Labouvie-Vief captures the spirit of this inquiry:

> While the theme of youth is flexibility, the hallmark of adulthood is commitment and responsibility. Careers must be started, intimacy bonds formed, children raised. In short, in a world of a multitude of logical possibilities, one course of action must be adopted. This conscious commitment to one pathway and the deliberate disregard of other logical choices may mark the onset of adult cognitive maturity. . . .
>
> The pure logic of youth may, of course, serve local or temporary adaptive value, and therefore its importance should not be denigrated. It permits a circulatory exercise of operatory schemes that are to be put to pragmatic use later on. It thus helps to guarantee the flexibility demanded of mature adult adaptation. This is our first proposed conclusion: adulthood brings structural change, not just in the perfection of logic, but in its reintegration with pragmatic necessities [Labouvie-Vief, 1980c, p. 153].

The need to take into account pragmatic necessities may thus require the ability to tolerate contradiction and ambiguity, which, according to Riegel, is a feature of adult thought:

> The mature person needs to achieve a new apprehension and an effective use of contradictions in operations and thoughts. Contradictions should no longer be regarded as deficiencies that have to be straightened out by formal thinking but, in a confirmative manner, as the very basis of all activities. In particular, they form the basis for any innovative and creative work. Adulthood and maturity represent the period in life during which the individual knowingly reappraises the role of formal, i.e. non-contradictory, thought and during

which he may succeed again (as the young child has unknowingly succeeded in his "primitive dialectic") to accept contradictions in his actions and thoughts ("scientific dialectic") [1975, p. 101].

In the above examples, the formal operational period is deemed to be limited by its abstractness and removal from everyday problem-posing and solving. This type of reasoning is correctly applied to a very narrow range of problems but can play only a subordinate role in efforts to solve the concrete problems of adult life.

Both the psychometric (intelligence-testing) and cognitive-structuralist traditions, then, seem to be converging on the view that intellectual and cognitive growth occurs in the adult years and that this growth is based on the experience of dealing with concrete problems and situations at work, in the home, and in community life. In both traditions, there is a move away from what might be called academic problem solving and toward everyday problem solving.

A number of research programs have now emerged in response to this development (see Baltes, 1987; Rybash, Hoyer, and Roodin, 1986). They focus on areas of growth in the second half of life—growth in wisdom (Dittman-Kohli and Baltes, 1986; Dittman-Kohli, 1985; Smith, 1988; Sternberg, 1990a), expertise (Denney, 1979; Hoyer, 1985), relativistic thinking (Sinnott, 1984; Benack, 1984), problem finding (Arlin, 1975, 1984), dialectical thinking (Basseches, 1980, 1984), and everyday thinking (Rogoff and Lave, 1984). The research efforts are still in their infancy. However, they do focus our attention on the continuing and highly varied growth of intellectual and cognitive capacity during the adult years. It is significant that this growth is predicated on experience and measured in contexts with a high degree of real-life complexity.

Academic and Everyday Problem Solving

To conclude this review of adult intelligence, we would like to explore the differences between typical test problems and the problems people encounter at work and in the course of family and community life. Many adult educators regard formal testing procedures as antithetical to the development and maintenance of a supportive learning environment, but the question of testing adults cannot be ignored, because so many sponsors of adult education insist on competency-based training methods and attempt to introduce promotion on the basis of formal appraisals. What, then, is the difference between formal test questions and everyday, informal problems? Further, is this difference relevant to a better understanding of adult intelligence? Sternberg (1990b) certainly believes that academic and everyday problems are different and that the difference is important for understanding adult intelligence. Neisser (1976) and Gardner (1985a) express similar views. The following discussion of the range of ways in which the two kinds of problems differ owes a great deal to Sternberg's insights.

Problem Recognition and Definition

Written tests pose problems in very specific ways. Once a person understands the test format, there is no ambiguity about what is a problem or when it needs to be solved—it is right here, right now. By contrast, the ability to recognize and anticipate problems before they strike is a key skill in the world of work, allowing the development of contingency plans: How will a particular product be affected by an increase in sales tax or import duty? How will it be affected by a rise in the cost of maintenance and repair? This ability to *find* problems—that is, to define ill-structured or unstated problems—has been documented elsewhere (Arlin, 1986, 1990).

In addition, test problems generally include instructions about the parameters of the problem: what it does and does not include, and what to assume about the background of the problem. This definition channels the problem solver in a certain direction—the direction being tested. In the everyday world, problem definition is much more open ended. If, for example, a child persistently disrupts the family's evening meal by behaving badly and refusing to eat, the "problem" can be defined in a myriad of ways: Whose problem is it? What aspects of the situation promote the misbehavior? (That is, Is the meal late or early? Is it always at the same time? Is the television on? What are the seating arrangements? Are table manners stressed? Does the child know what is expected? What conversation occurs? Who cooks the meal? Who talks to whom? What is the cuisine? Is the cuisine predictable or unpredictable? Is homework completed before or after the evening meal?) Depending on the answers to questions such as these, the problem may be defined as having to do with parental authority, competition between siblings, adjustment to schoolwork, overstimulation, tiredness, and so on. The point is that the definition of the problem is wide open, and thus the possibilities for action are many.

Number of "Correct" Answers

Intelligence tests typically have a single correct or best answer. In everyday life, the solution must often be found among several possibilities. For example, the decision on where to buy or rent a home involves a sophisticated analysis of the needs and resources of the people involved. There are many possible selection factors, all of differing value to different households: public transportation, police, and school systems; tax rates; aesthetic appeal; price; access to services; and so on. To add to the complexity of the problem, there is no absolute scale for comparing quality in one factor with deficiency in another, or even, in many cases, for making a clear judgment on how one home compares to another on a single factor. Invariably, such an analysis leads to a range of choices (for those of us who are fortunate enough to have a choice in such matters) rather than a single solution. In addition, such decisions are often made on the basis of questions that have no apparent relationship to the matter at hand. To continue the illustration, one may decide not to purchase or rent a particular dwelling simply because one does not like the "feel" of the neighborhood! This can hardly be considered a "wrong" answer, because such feelings are real and tangible to the people concerned.

Access to Complete Information

Test problems typically include all the information to solve each problem. By contrast, in everyday life some significant information is usually missing. Nonetheless, adults must act in the world—make a decision or commit to a particular course—regardless of the gaps in their knowledge. Indeed, occasionally conflicting pieces of information must be evaluated and acted upon. This ability to cope with limited, ambiguous, or conflicting information is arguably a characteristic of adult intelligence, and particularly in such milieus as the business world, where the range of inputs is vast and the degree of control exercised by any one individual is limited. A flood or coup in one country, for example, can send futures prices soaring in another. Such scenarios demand the ability to make the best possible decision—given the information available—and the intuitive wit to protect oneself from extreme losses in an unforeseen crisis. It is no wonder that faced with the breadth of the unknown in business, students consistently complain that university or business school is no preparation for the real world!

Context

Problems on tests are typically decontextualized, whereas everyday problems are contextualized. By *contextualized,* we mean that all the operating variables have to be taken into account when approaching the solution—none can be assumed to be constants. Real-world problems can't escape such issues as why the problem is seen as important, who will benefit from the solution, and what events led up to the problem. As an example, in facing the question of how to deal with a young person "at risk," a welfare worker must take into account the complete background of the case. The analysis would include everything from the caregiver's housekeeping habits through to issues such as drug or alcohol dependence, relationships with siblings, progress at school, the history and nature of the risk, and the likelihood and timing of a satisfactory resolution of the matters at hand. In such case scenarios, problems cannot be fruitfully approached without a detailed understanding of context. In a very real sense, there is no such thing as a theoretical understanding of at-risk youth; the problem simply does not exist out of context.

Feedback

The feedback from test problems is usually quite unambiguous. Test questions typically have one correct answer, so much so that many tests are designed to be marked electronically. By contrast, everyday life rarely provides explicit feedback on performance—unless, of course, it is unusually poor or excellent. One of the skills we develop in adult life is to learn to operate with incomplete or unclear feedback on our performance. We learn at an early age that being told we are good at something can mean anything from total satisfaction on the part of the speaker to complete lack of interest, and that the accomplishment itself may be merely a rest stop on the road to the speaker's true goal for us: excellence! At work and at home, we continue throughout our lives to face the same kind of mixed or partial responses to our actions. The mature adult learns to live with ambiguity and lack of clarity.

Social Context

Test problems are usually solved alone. On the other hand, everyday problems must often be solved in conjunction with other people. The workplace frequently presents such problems. When more than one solution is possible, there are bound to be competing interests—and the solution finally adopted may be the one with greatest support from colleagues, not the one meeting some abstract ideal of "best." Working in groups is now recognized as an intellectual ability, and one that is increasingly valued by employers. Whereas once management theory encouraged individualism and the use of internal competition to boost overall output, new developments, including the rise of Total Quality Management and the introduction of flatter structures and self-managing work groups, have inspired renewed interest in collaborative problem solving. We have also witnessed the recent rise of interest in what is termed the learning organization. In such situations, a high individual IQ score or the ability to excel in abstract problem solving will not necessarily be of more value than skills in listening, teamwork, and group creativity.

The overriding point Sternberg is making is that real-life problem solving is by nature a far more open system than that found in the traditional school or college environment. Ambiguity, poor feedback, unclear problem boundaries, the vagaries of the relationships we have with others, and many other factors all combine to constitute the very loose framework of our adult experience of intelligent action in the everyday world. Such a conclusion would reflect the experience of many adult educators, especially those involved in facilitation or development work, where simplistic answers to complex, multilayered situations such as poverty, unemployment, or low student self-esteem are of little use.

Conclusion

In contemporary theory and research on the nature of intelligence during the adult years, there is a growing recognition that development is based upon the expertise gained from dealing with concrete problems and situations at work, in the home, and in community life. Recent reconceptualizations of intelligence reinforce the view that it can only be fully understood by examining how it is applied in the everyday world. It is no longer deemed sufficient to measure an individual's "computational power"; it is also important to assess how this power is directed or exploited (Sternberg, 1984a, 1988b). Conventional intelligence tests, with their emphasis on basic cognitive skills and formal logic, are no longer seen as appropriate for all tasks in adult life; this is clearly made apparent in our detailed examination of the nature of the formal problems framed in conventional tests. A similar trend has emerged in the literature on cognitive development, which is increasingly viewing adulthood as bringing with it new forms of thinking and reasoning associated with distinctly adult life tasks. The implications for adult education are important. First, adulthood can now be legitimately viewed, not as a period of intellectual stability or decline but as a period of ongoing intellectual and cognitive growth, qualitatively different from childhood. Second, because this growth is largely based on accumulated life experiences, the capacity to utilize experience for learning and for building expertise becomes a central concern for adult education. Of course, the notion of experience as a basis for learning has been a feature of adult education theory and practice for some time. However, we can now link this idea to a body of literature dealing with adult intelligence and cognition and explore the results of research into the development of practical intelligence and expertise throughout the life course.

Chapter Three

Practical Intelligence and the Development of Expertise

In the previous chapter, we considered the literature on IQ and cognitive structualism and explored various views of the nature of intelligence through the life course. We also introduced a discussion of the differences between academic and practical problem solving. In this chapter we pursue further the idea of the practical/academic divide through a formal review of the growing body of research on the development of practical intelligence and expertise among adults. As little of this work is available in adult education sources, we believe that our tour of the literature and analysis of its implications for adult education practice will prove worthwhile.

Interest in practical as opposed to academic intelligence has its source partly in the disquiet felt about the limitations of standard intelligence tests, and partly in the observation that many people who are not in conventional terms academically successful or "intelligent" do manage to negotiate their own paths through the world and to master any topic that interests them. These people have a practical rather than theoretical bent, and until fairly recent times, their success was for the large part not recognized as a form of intelligence by educators and psychologists. Those who did take note of it usually relegated it to the second rank of importance, marginalizing it in a world fascinated by conventional intellectual brilliance. This devaluation of practical ability has a long history, originating in the writings of the Greek philosophers and propagated by their heirs for almost two and a half thousand years.

The development of tests of intelligence reinforced the bias toward those who can successfully manipulate the theoretical problems typically posed in IQ tests, which are by nature stripped of everyday context and presented in a formal educational setting. A student's academic and thus personal future can be determined by scores achieved on intelligence tests, which become more or less permanently enshrined in a global IQ measure. This is still the case despite doubts expressed almost from the beginning of formal intelligence testing as to the true meaning and veracity of IQ as a measure of human intellectual potential, and despite a myriad of formal studies pointing to a range of theoretical problems and cultural and other biases inherent in many IQ tests. For most of the history of the intelligence testing movement, there was no empirical evidence to support alternative or even complementary cognitive constructs other than that purported to be measured by IQ tests. In the last twenty years, however, interest has grown in alternative views. As we noted in the previous chapter, the results of empirical studies into such previously taboo subjects as wisdom, problem finding, expertise, relativistic thinking, dialectical thinking, practical or everyday intelligence, tacit knowledge, creativity, and insight have served to redress the balance and call into question previous assumptions concerning the nature and character of intelligence. Interest in these new constructs has created something of a crisis in terminology. For most of this century, the term "intelligence" was closely identified with whatever it was that IQ tests measured, and both theorists and empirical researchers must now struggle to describe the newly developing constructs. Some writers have chosen to retain the conventional term—intelligence—and explicitly or implicitly redefine it in a broader, more inclusive sense, while others have abandoned the word completely.

The common thread in all such studies and theoretical writings is the belief in and search for qualities known as intelligences, competencies, or abilities that may be, or at least appear to be, independent from so-called academic intelligence. What distinguishes most research in this area is an interest in the everyday or real-life settings outside the psychological laboratory or formal classroom. This move sees studies becoming increasingly focused on particular professions—restaurant workers, canoe-builders, magistrates, chess-players—or particular functions such as decision making and problem solving in everyday milieus.

To establish a context for the contemporary work on practical intelligence and expertise, this chapter commences with an overview of the historical distinctions between the theoretical and the practical in Western culture. We argue that the distinction between academic and nonacademic intelligence is part of this history. Then we present and examine various models of the nature and development of practical intelligence and expertise, and discuss the part tacit knowledge appears to play in both practical intelligence and expertise. It is our argument that adult intelligence and cognitive development can be reconceptualized as comprising both practical intelligence and expertise. Such a reconceptualization should not be understood as excluding IQ or indeed any number of other cognitive constructs. Rather, we believe that adulthood can be reframed from this perspective in such a way as to shed light on adult development and adult learning.

The Practical and the Theoretical in Western Culture

The discontinuity between academic and nonacademic intelligence, be it expressed philosophically, practically, or theologically, has existed in Western culture since 400 B.C. Discussions of intelligence regularly start from the presupposition that there is a divide between practical ("hands on") activities, and theoretical thought or contemplation—the latter typically carrying more prestige than the former. Many examples of this attitude are cited by Hooykaas (1972), whose work we turn to for much of this analysis.

Historically, Western culture has taken a lower view of manual work than of cognitive activity. Among the ancient Greek philosophers and leaders, Hycurgus forbade the citizens of Sparta to occupy themselves with trades. Herodotus wrote that both Greeks and barbarians looked upon artisans as inferior. Idealistic Athenian philosophers maintained that the intellectual and spiritual development necessary for running the state "could not take place in conjunction with manual work" (Hooykaas, 1972, p. 76). Although Plato considered agriculture to be the basis of life in his ideal state, he said the manual labor connected with it should be left to slaves. Aristotle supported the idea that the nomad, fisher, and hunter lived "natural lives," yet despised commerce.

Of all human activities, Aristotle saw contemplation as the highest, for it had a purpose within itself and existed for its own sake. Practical arts, on the contrary, looked for some advantage outside their own activity (Aristotle, *Nicomachean Ethics* X, 8,7).

The Roman philosopher Cicero thought artisans performed vulgar and sordid work; a mechanical workshop, he wrote, "contains nothing fit for a freeborn man" (Cicero, *De Officius*, i, 42).

Plato believed the arithmetical study of numbers to be a lofty and philosophical occupation—but calculation to be vulgar, for the use of merchants and retail traders (Hooykaas, 1972). As to geometry, Plato also expressed his disapproval; there were too many terms that reminded one of manual work: "their language smells of slavery."

According to Hooykaas, this low view of manual labor and even of the work of the artisan passed over into Christendom via Platonism and Aristotelianism.

In the realm of science, some experiments with material things were carried out in the Middle Ages, but theory generally held sway. In 1338, for example, Thomas Bradwardine asserted that a magnet with iron hanging on it does not weigh more than one without it, "as experience teaches us" (Hooykaas, 1972, p. 85). Albertus Magnus (1193–1280) once dismissed an opponent with the damning epithet that he was "a mechanic, not a philosopher" (cited in Hooykaas, 1972, p. 88).

Things changed with the Renaissance, when theoretical reason began to lose ground in the battle with observation and experience. For example, Scholastic philosophers had "proved" that heat made human life impossible in the world's tropical zones. As world exploration developed, there was great resistance to the information about tropical civilizations presented by explorers returning from voyages to these areas—after all, they were but artisans, engineers, mariners, and pilots: "uneducated" men who knew little Latin and lacked university education (Hooykaas, 1972). Lamoens, a sixteenth-century Portuguese poet, wrote in support of these "ignorant" men (cited in Hooykaas, 1972, p. 37). "I have seen things of which the uneducated mariners, who only have long experience as their teacher, proclaim the truth—whereas scholars, who judge by science and pure reason only, demonstrate that they are not true or misunderstood."

Joâ de Castro remarked that the inhabitability of the tropical zone had once appeared against reason, but now "it seems the most reasonable thing in the world" (Cited in Hooykaas, 1972, p. 38).

Part of the reason that the work of artisans was looked down upon was the belief, expounded by idealistic philosophers, that competing with nature was illegitimate. Hooykaas notes (p. 56): "The artificial was considered inferior to the natural, even from a moral point of view. This was emphasised in stories about the Golden Age, when man still lived soberly and, as Seneca would have it, without architects, carpenters and weavers, or as Lucretius thought, even without agriculture, and when everybody was happy and contented."

Nevertheless, as the Renaissance progressed, there was increasing encouragement to observe, visit workshops, and learn from the common person. For example, Cromwell's army chaplain, John Webster, demanded the provision of laboratories as well as libraries in the universities, "so that young people would not be trained entirely in empty speculations."

The exaltation of the theoretical or contemplative over the practical continued well into the modern period. Shapin and Barnes (1976) traced such beliefs in various writings on English education published between 1770 and 1850, much of which contributed to the discontinuity between the academic and practical spheres. During this period, the debate was largely about mental types, usually expressed in terms of a dichotomy between the "higher orders" and the "lower ranks." They identified three such dichotomies. The first set the *sensual* and *concrete* character of thought of the lower ranks against the *intellectual, verbal,* and *abstract* qualities of the upper ranks. An anonymous commentator of the time (known only as a "Country Gentleman") describes the lower orders as follows (cited in Shapin and Barnes, 1976, p. 232): "It may easily be shown that practice and theory seldom unite in the same individual; that the occupation of the practitioner requires all his time and thoughts to fulfil the wishes of eye or hand: whilst the theorist reasons within himself, and throws himself on his mind. Theoretical excellence must have reason for its soil, which mechanics have not."

The second dichotomy was that between the *simplicity* of the thought of the lower classes and the *complexity* of that of their betters. The third dichotomy concerned the *active use* of knowledge and experience by the higher orders as opposed to the *passive* and *automatic* way the lower ranks reacted to experience. The authors also note the continuing influence of Plato and Aristotle on the framing of all three views of mental types. Such views on the nature of lower class talents and pursuits strongly affected both the type and extent of the educational opportunities extended to them. Rosenstock (1991) continues the same debate in a manner that would lead us to believe little has changed over the years. He claims that in contemporary U.S. high schools: "Head and Hand have never been further apart. . . . Vocational students are relegated to 'working with their hands', with minimal and diluted academic content, as the system fulfils its prophecy of their limited potential" (p. 435). The twenty-five-hundred-year pattern of discrimination against those who work with their hands has recently been heightened in some nations though government policy shifts toward the national implementation of competency-based training. Hager and Gonczi (1993, p. 40) comment on the Australian situation:

> The pervasive influence of the vocational/general dichotomy has
> been a marked feature of the competency debate as it has unfolded

in Australia. As the debate has clearly demonstrated, the thinking of many people in the educational sector is dominated by the traditional dichotomy between vocational education and 'genuine' education and all that this entails, viz. body vs. mind, hand vs. head, manual vs. mental, skills vs. knowledge, applied vs. pure, knowing how vs. knowing that, practice vs. theory, particular vs. general, and training vs. education. Chipman (1992) is, we believe, correct in tracing back to Socrates the influence of these dichotomies on our educational thinking.

In education and training, then, we still see the outworkings of the ancient prejudice favoring the *thinker* over the *doer*. As Hager and Gonczi state, the argument can be framed in any one of a number of dichotomies, but it remains the same argument.

In summary, Western culture has had a historical propensity to distinguish the practical from the theoretical, and those who work with their hands from those who work with their minds. Horowitz (1975, pp. 398–399) describes the "head" position as follows: "Those who work with their minds are more important than those who work with their physical power. In assessing the importance of people, one must distinguish those who can from those who cannot dialecticize."

Our argument is that there has been a historical bias toward the abstract over the practical in Western culture and that a contemporary corollary of this is the exaltation of academic intelligence over practical intelligence. Recent challenges to the latter view may prove very important to the field of adult education.

The Concept of Practical Intelligence and Expertise

There have been a number of attempts to define the concept of practical intelligence. Sternberg and Caruso (1985), for example, characterize practical knowledge as being procedural, not declarative, and as relevant to everyday life. Ford (1986) emphasizes that practical intelligence has external goals:

- The goals to be accomplished must be transitional—that is, they must refer to an effect outside of the person (fixing a flat tire, controlling someone else's behavior), rather than an effect inside the person (understanding a concept, experiencing a sunset).

- The goals to be accomplished must be important either to the individual being assessed or to the cultural groups of which the individual is a part.

Walters and Gardner (1986) define intelligence so as to include practical intelligence:

- Intelligence is an ability or set of abilities that permits an individual to solve problems or fashion products of consequence in a particular cultural setting.

- All intelligent acts are potentially practical, and those practical activities that involve solving problems or creating products, require at least one intelligence.

In summary, the terminology used to describe practical or nonacademic intelligence emphasizes practice as opposed to theory, direct usefulness as opposed to intellectual curiosity, procedural usefulness as opposed to declarative knowledge, and commonplace, everyday action or thought with immediate, visible consequences. Practical thinking thus has a real-life end in mind: it seeks to do, to move, to achieve something outside of itself, and works toward that purpose.

Case Study: The "Milk Factory Studies" of Sylvia Scribner—the Practical Dimension in Action

One of the relatively rare attempts to systematically study real-life, practical thinking was undertaken by Sylvia Scribner, a cross-cultural psychologist who published a number of papers probing the cognitive abilities of traditional peoples. Much of her approach is thus drawn from this genre, and the acute awareness of the limitations of standard measures of intelligence in cross-cultural studies informs her work. The Milk Factory Studies, so named because they took place in a large dairy processing plant in the United States, have generated great interest in a variety of circles including cognitive psychology, education, and adult education. Her research results are recorded in Scribner, 1984a, 1984b, 1986, and Scribner and Fahrmeier, 1982. Both the results and the research methods employed are significant for adult education, so we will consider this set of studies in detail.

A number of researchers have put forward psychological constructs of practical intelligence as an underlying ability or structure of intelligence, but Scribner makes no such claims. She prefers to concentrate her work on the idea of practical thought as a dynamic process rather than a cognitive construct:

> My notion of practical thinking can be glossed as "mind in action".
> I use the term to refer to thinking that is embedded in the larger
> purposive activities of daily life and that functions to achieve the
> goals of those activities. Active goals may involve mental accomplishments or manual accomplishments . . . but whatever their
> nature, practical thinking is instrumental to their achievement. So
> conceived—as embedded and instrumental—practical thinking
> stands in contrast to the type of thinking involved in performance
> of isolated mental tasks undertaken as ends in themselves [Scribner,
> 1986, p. 15].

Scribner contrasts practical thought with academic, formal, and theoretical thought. Thus she sets herself firmly in a tradition of describing practical thought and intelligence as: *not* academic or formal, but goal directed, problem oriented, and directed outside the individual.

The framework of practical thinking that Scribner developed was the result of more than two years of research work in a milk processing plant situated in a large eastern U.S. city. The plant employed some three hundred workers in a range of job categories. (Scribner, 1984a, p. 4). The aim of the project was: "to contribute to a functional theory of practical thinking and to test a research strategy for its investigation" (Scribner, 1984a, p. 2).

Cognitive research in everyday environments is fraught with methodological and practical difficulties. In an attempt to eliminate the problems generated by what she terms "the rigor-relevance controversy over the relevance of descriptive versus explanatory approaches" (that is, observational versus experimental research methods), Scribner and her team evolved a three-phase research strategy.

The first phase was ethnographic in approach and included formal observation, informal chats, formal interviews, and casual observation. The results were then used to generate hypotheses about "factors that might be regulating variability and about the features distinguishing skilled and novice problem solving." Second, job simulations were developed to test and explore hypotheses under more controlled conditions. Finally, a series of experiments were devised using formal laboratory techniques. The aim of this third stage was to "probe questions on a more specific level of analysis than simulation studies made possible: how workers organize their job knowledge . . . [and] change their representations of objects used in the work environments as they acquire experience" (Scribner, 1984a, p. 4). Scribner notes that these procedures were invented for the task at hand and were somewhat ad hoc (her words) in character.

Her team examined four types of jobs: product assembly, wholesale delivery, inventory, and clerical office work. To examine expert/novice distinctions, workers were rotated between jobs. For example, expert product assemblers (packers) became novice inventory clerks. In addition, a number of school students at grade 9 level (broadly equivalent to the education level of most of the blue-collar workers at the plant), were also used in simulations.

Scribner's studies resulted in a challenging formulation of

thought in context. She developed a five-part model of practical thinking, the characteristics of which are described below:

Flexibility

According to Scribner, practical thinking is marked by *flexibility*— solving the same problem in different ways, with each way finely fitted to the particular occasion on hand. Drawing on expert/novice comparisons, Scribner notes that novices tended to rely on algorithms that produced correct solutions via repeated application of a single problem procedure. Experts, in contrast, displayed a repertoire of solution modes fitted to the properties of specific problems in changing task environments. This view of problem solving differs from more formal models, which by contrast "lead us to expect that repetitive problems or problems of the same logical class will be solved by the same sequence of operations (algorithms) on all occasions of their presentation" (Scribner, 1986, p. 22).

What makes these claims original is that they are based on analysis, job simulation, and experiments on repetitive, blue-collar tasks such as product assembly, inventory, and pricing—not on formal testing in educational or research environments. It was found that subjects did not employ variable methods on a trial and error basis. Experts consistently scored very high in accuracy: way beyond what could be expected from a basic chance relationship.

Fine-Tuning the Problem-Solving System to the Environment

Of this second characteristic, Scribner writes, "Skilled problem-solving in the dairy was finely tuned to the properties of the external material environment and to changing conditions within it" (Scribner, 1984a, p. 38).

That is, skilled practical thinking draws aspects of the given environment, be they people, things, or information, into the problem-solving system. The physical environment does not determine the problem-solving process; instead, it is drawn into the process through worker initiative.

Scribner contrasts her view with two other theoretical positions. She points out that cognitive theories built upon the computer metaphor view the world as "a stage on which actors execute the outcomes of their mental operations" (Scribner, 1986, p. 23). On the other hand, contextualist theories view the environment as a context, an external envelope, affecting cognitive process largely through interpretive procedures, while the task remains a unit that can be moved from context to context without changing its nature. Counting sheep, for example, is the same task as counting people, only the unit being counted has changed. In contrast to the computer metaphor and the contextualist theories, skilled practical thinking emphasizes the inextricability of task from environment, and the continual interplay between internal representation and operations and external reality throughout the course of the problem-solving process (Scribner, 1986, p. 23).

For example, counting routines in situ were found to be precisely adapted to the shape of things to be counted: stacks five high prompted counting by fives; six high, counting by sixes. Further, experienced drivers modified their arithmetic operations and problem formulation depending on whether they had on hand pocket calculators or pencil and paper. Workers even made mental tools of the environment—a stack of dairy cases becoming a counting unit, for example.

In summary, for Scribner, "environment includes all social, symbolic and material resources outside the head of the individual problem solver" (Scribner, 1986, p. 25).

Economy

Scribner found that effective problem solvers designed strategies to save effort wherever possible. She sees this effort saving as a higher-order thinking strategy, which entails the "psychological reorganization of work tasks to reduce the number of physical or mental steps required for their accomplishment and/or to simplify steps that cannot be eliminated; it has nothing to do with efficiency of movement or other industrial engineering concepts" (Scribner, 1984a, p. 39).

In the dairy, least-effort strategies were acknowledged as cultural norms. Individuals often explicitly described their active search for shortcuts or easier ways to do a job. Product assemblers reformulated orders to save physical moves; inventory staff constructed mental representations for arrays that enabled substitution of shortcutting arithmetic procedures for lengthy processes of enumeration. In a novice/expert job simulation, Scribner found that students did acquire least-effort strategies as a result of practice alone, without any formal instruction. On the first trial, optimal solutions for students were at a chance level; by the fourth, 79 percent of student problem solutions conformed to the least-effort principle (Scribner, 1984a, p. 13).

As far as product assembly was concerned, the following guidelines held: the choice of solution mode was regulated by a criterion of least physical effort, and extra mental effort was extended where necessary to save physical effort.

When asked why they adopted least-effort techniques, workers responded consistently and to the point: "We want to save our backs" (Scribner, 1984a, p.12)

Dependency on Setting-Specific Knowledge

One of the consistent results of expertise studies has been the close correlation between expert performance and a high level of domain-specific or setting-specific knowledge. Scribner reinforces this point forcefully as it pertains to the dairy: "The hallmark of expert problem-solving lay in the fact that the experienced worker was able to use specific dairy and job related knowledge to generate flexible and economical solution procedures. Expert problem solving procedures were content-infused, not content free" (Scribner, 1984a, p. 39).

The knowledge that workers needed was both vast and trivial, depending on the task. For example, when asked about the price of particular items, many delivery drivers said that they did not handle the product in question—not that they did not know the price. (That is, they asserted that it was outside their knowledge domain.) As to written documentation, workers could often answer questions only about the part of a form they had to complete, and were unfamiliar with the meanings of many label headings or other items they did not use. Another factor Scribner mentions is what she terms "the saliency of knowledge" for accomplishment of activity goals (Scribner, 1984a, p. 40). Workers organized their knowledge along dimensions that made a difference to their job functions. Warehouse workers—whose job was to locate products—used product location in the warehouse as a classification. On the other hand, clerks—who were responsible for filing—relied on kind of dairy product as their main taxonomic principle.

Problem Formation

The category of problem formation was not explicitly referred to in Scribner, 1984a, but did appear in Scribner, 1986. By problem formation, Scribner refers to the process of *formulating* problems as opposed to simply solving them. Formal problem-solving models, she suggests, see problems as given, the intellectual work consisting of selecting and executing a series of steps which will lead to a solution (Scribner, 1986, p. 21). In contrast, practical thinking actually reformulates or redefines problems. Problems were recast in the dairy: unit price problems into case price problems, "take away" problems into "add on" problems (for example, converting 16–6=10 into 8+2=10), and counting problems into multiplication problems.

Scribner's work on practical intelligence is located firmly in a research movement that attempts to identify the features of adult intelligence and thinking, especially as it is manifested at work. Also within this movement are a number of studies specifically focusing on the concept of expertise. It is to these we now turn.

Studies of Expertise

Practical intelligence, when applied in the context of a particular domain of work or knowledge, is often referred to as expertise. Many of the studies of expertise have been conducted independently of any theory of adult development. In some domains (such as sports, chess, and music), expertise can develop at a young age. In other domains, expertise can only develop over a lifetime of experience (for example, in professions such as law, medicine, architecture, and teaching). Nevertheless, there is a shared presupposition that expertise is built upon the knowledge and skill gained through sustained practice and experience. In all areas, studies seek to document the performance capabilities or qualities of the expert. Not surprisingly, the most common technique is to contrast the performance of experts with those of novices with a view to developing a model of the nature of expertise. This contrast is accomplished through a variety of techniques—simulations (Lawrence, 1988), naturalistic observation (Scribner, 1986), perceptions of what constitutes expertise (Ford, 1986), structured tasks of some kind (Chase and Simon, 1973; Ceci and Liker, 1986; Gentner, 1988), or verbal articulation of expert judgment (Schmidt, Norman, and Boshuizen, 1990). Some of these studies are described here to provide a context for the following discussion.

One of the earliest studies on expertise focused on chess playing. Chase and Simon (1973), extending the previous work of De Groot (1966), confirmed that chess masters could reproduce the configurations of pieces on a chess board almost perfectly after only five seconds of viewing. However, they were no better at this task than novices when the pieces were placed randomly and without regard to any sensible rules of chess. The experts displayed superior memory only when the chess pieces were arranged in a meaningful way. Chase and Simon sought to explain how the chess masters managed to "chunk" together clusters of pieces and therefore reduce short-term memory load. From the point of view of subsequent investigations of expertise, however, the significance of this study is that the superior memory of the experts was clearly specific to the domain that was meaningful to them matching Scribner's fourth characteristic of practical intelligence. Studies such as these helped to support the notion that the performance of subjects on various memory and problem-solving tasks may have more to do with their knowledge base than with their generic memory or problem-solving abilities.

Spilich (1979) compared experts and nonexperts in baseball (that is, those possessing a high or low level of knowledge). After hearing the text of a half-inning account of a fictitious baseball game, subjects were asked to summarize the content. Analysis indicated qualitative and quantitative differences in recall for high- and low-knowledge subjects. High-knowledge subjects showed greater ability to relate the actions of the game to the goal structure and to maintain the most important knowledge in a working memory system.

Myles-Worsley and Johnston (1988) compared recognition memory skills for chest X-ray films using experienced and inexperienced radiologists as subjects. Memory for abnormal X-ray films increased with experience—but memory for normal films decreased with experience, indicating that experts could sift rapidly through irrelevant information and proceed directly to the key point. In the case of radiologists, this means speedily and accurately identifying abnormal rather than normal features.

Ceci and Liker (1986) framed their study of racetrack handicapping to explore the relationship between so-called academic and nonacademic intelligence. Their subjects were similar in background and experience to those Scribner employed. In the words of the researchers, "Our subjects were quite unlike the ubiquitous college freshman upon whom most models of intelligence have been based. Subjects in this study were middle aged and older men who were ardent horse racing fans. On average these men had been attending horse races at least twice per week during the sixteen years preceding the start of this study" (p. 174). They found that there was no correlation between successful handicapping (that is, the ability to predict probable favorites) and IQ (Wechsler Adult Intelligence Scale). However, they then proceeded to examine the complexity of racetrack handicapping. They argued that racetrack handicappers need to deal with twenty to thirty categories of information about each entry (things like the horse's lifetime speed, the jockey's ability, and the size of the track), with between three and twenty-nine levels for each category. They asked both experts and novices to predict the winner and odds of fifty hypothetically constructed two-horse races (in each case a standard horse was compared with a horse uniquely described for that race). From earlier interviews they hypothesized that the handicappers considered the interaction of a range of variables in coming to their decision. This was confirmed: "Experts appeared to assess the unique variance associated with each level of a given variable then proceeded to qualify this contribution through its interactions with other variables and groups of variables. For nonexperts each variable was considered independently for its unique contribution to the horse's chances of winning. . . . [Experts] go beyond the raw data in the racing program, assigning 'weights' to each variable, systematically combining the various variables (sic) in complex non additive ways, and computing a rough odds/probability equivalent for each horse" (pp. 130–132). They make a compelling case for their conclusion that racetrack handicapping is as intellectually demanding as the decision making apparent among established professions such as science, law, and banking. They interpret the finding of no correlation between this ability and IQ as evidence that IQ should not be generalized to nonacademic tasks and contexts.

Development of Practical Intelligence and Expertise

What is the source of this nonacademic or practical intelligence? Ceci and Liker dismiss the possibility that it is based solely on a mental template of a winning horse's profile built up from past experience, as they would find it difficult to attach the label "intelligence" to such a process. However, others have argued that this is precisely how experience operates to produce expertise. This is the position adopted by Schmidt, Norman, and Boshuizen (1990), who focus on medical expertise. They point out that problem-solving and problem-based learning approaches in medical education assume that clinical skills essentially consist of domain-independent reasoning skills or heuristics. However, they cite studies examining the nature of clinical competence which show that performance on problems is content-specific, that is, problem-solving performance is dependent on the availability of knowledge relevant to a particular problem. A second assumption in medical education is that experts will gather more data, or at least more critical or essential data, than novices. Once again, this cannot be substantiated in the literature. In their own study of expert and novice diagnostic protocols, they argue that expertise develops from a "conceptually rich and rational knowledge base to one comprised of largely experiential and non-analytical instances" (p. 619). They propose a four-stage theory of the development of clinical expertise, as described below.

Stage 1: Elaborated Causal Networks

Novices explain the causes and consequences of disease in terms of underlying pathophysiological processes which become increasingly elaborated and complex with learning. They have only a limited understanding of how disease manifests itself in reality, and a prototypical perspective on disease.

Stage 2: Abridged Causal Networks

"By applying his knowledge he begins to take certain short cuts in his reasoning. . . . He will no longer have to activate all possible relevant knowledge in order to understand what is going on in his patient; only knowledge pertinent to understanding the case will be activated" (p. 614).

Stage 3: Emergence of Illness Scripts

"By meeting many patients the student gets a feeling of how disease manifestations vary. . . . Gradually, illness scripts for different diseases develop" (p. 614).

"An illness script in its most general format is a grammar that provides rules enabling one to construct mental models of a family of diseases" (p. 615). Thus problem solving in routine cases is a matter of script searching, selection, and verification. There is evidence that illness scripts assist to organize information in memory—they are also highly idiosyncratic and bear only a superficial relation to prototypical cases as they occur in textbooks.

Stage 4: Storing Patient Encounters as Instance Scripts

"Expert clinical reasoning is based on the similarity between the presenting situation and some previous patient available from memory. . . . We suggest that this availability of a store of possibly hundreds or thousands of previous patients is not simply an interesting curiosity but is instead a central feature of expertise in medicine" (p. 617).

Implications of the Four-Stage Model

The interesting aspect of this model of expertise is that it contrasts sharply with the idea that experts work at a deeper level of processing. Schmidt and colleagues argue that expertise is largely non-analytical and based strongly on prior instances: "expertise is associated with a qualitative transition from a conceptually rich and rational knowledge base to one comprised of largely experiential and non-analytical instances" (p. 619). Thus the idea of developing general, explicit rules or principles of competence is peripheral to the essential components of expertise.

This contrasting point of view—especially if it is accepted on the evidence presented—raises the possibility that expertise is constituted differently in different domains. That is, expertise itself may only be properly understood in relation to a particular domain. This point is made by Lawrence (1988) in the introductory remarks to her study of judicial decision making. She argues that domain realism is important in the study of expertise, that is, expertise and the way it is studied should be pertinent to the domain in question. In the case of judicial decision making, the frame of reference that each magistrate brings to the procedure is an important influence. This includes such things as penal philosophy, views on the severity of the crime, concepts of the judicial role, and views on sentencing objectives. Thus expertise operates at the level of structuring (and awareness) of one's frame of reference. In addition, experts need to be able to understand and respond to environmental constraints such as legislated penalties, heavy caseloads, the law of evidence, and so on. Finally, expertise has to do with the ability to select information, draw inferences, and make sentencing decisions. Lawrence analyzed verbal protocols to determine differences between experts' and novices' handling of different cases. She concludes, "In a highly personalized professional role with individualized ways of defining outcomes and processes, experience provided the experts with patterns for reducing workloads. For these experts, experience also led to similar goals and perspectives on different types of offenses. Experience also brought with it ideas about what to look for and ways to follow up leads in the data" (pp. 256–257).

Lawrence's study illustrates how the concept of expertise becomes problematic in domains that are relatively ill-structured, that is, where there is considerable variation in the approach to a problem and its solution, and where the criteria for excellence are open to dispute. Such ill-structured domains are widespread in the world of work. As described earlier, even in such an apparently standardized and repetitive workplace as a dairy processing plant, Scribner (1986) found that experienced workers typically reformulated the problems presented to them and adopted flexible modes of solution appropriate to each occasion, principally for the purpose of achieving the most economical and least-effort solution to a problem.

Common Factors in Expertise

It may be true that a full understanding of expertise can only be achieved in relation to a particular domain. However, there are some common factors that cross domains. The best attempt at summarizing these to date is that of Chi, Glaser, and Farr (1988), as outlined below. (Other useful summaries can be found in Lesgold, 1984; Glaser, 1987, 1985; and Perkins and Salomon, 1989.)

Experts Excel Mainly in Their Own Domains. Experts have a good deal of domain knowledge upon which their expertise is built. This knowledge cannot easily be transferred to another domain.

Experts Perceive Large Meaningful Patterns in Their Domains. The organization of the knowledge base is such that "meaning" operates at a higher-order level (for example, lower-order data are chunked into meaningful wholes). This is illustrated in studies of chess (Chase and Simon, 1973), typing (Gentner, 1988), and taking inventory (Scribner, 1986).

Experts Are Faster and More Economical. They can often arrive at a solution without conducting an extensive search (Schmidt, Norman, and Boshuizen, 1990), and they are good at anticipating required actions and events (Gentner, 1988).

Experts Have Superior Memory. This capacity is restricted to a particular domain, though the domain itself may be "skilled memory." Expertise is restricted to the problem types encountered in experience. Memory capacity is considered by Schmidt, Norman, and Boshuizen (1990) to be the key to medical expertise. Nearly all investigations make some reference to the superior memory of experts. It appears that the phenomenon of chunking only partially explains this observation—even Chase and Simon (1973) observe that the master chess player recalls both larger chunks and *more* chunks (a finding they are at a loss to explain).

Experts See and Represent a Problem in Their Domain at a Deeper Level than Novices. Both experts and novices use conceptual categories, but those of the former are more "principled" or abstract. Certainly Ceci and Liker (1986) and even Gentner (1988) demonstrate this type of information organization. However, Schmidt, Norman, and Boshuizen (1990) cast some doubt on the point.

Experts Spend a Great Deal of Time Analyzing a Problem Qualitatively. That is, problem formation (see Scribner, 1986) is a feature of the way experts approach their task. This is especially the case with so-called ill-structured problems—for example, building a home or writing a piece of music or an essay—where the definition of the problem has a major impact on the content of the solution.

Experts Have Strong Self-Monitoring Skills. That is, they are aware of their errors and the need to reevaluate solutions, and they are more self-aware and alert to the complexity of the problems confronting them.

Much of the theory and research on expertise has been conducted with a view to reconceptualizing the nature of intelligence or building a cognitive model of expert problem solving. Dixon and Baltes (1986) consider expertise to be an aspect of the pragmatics of intelligence (see Chapter Two). The research on expertise is consistent with recent views of adult development in that it considers intelligence to be partly a system of factual and procedural knowledge, adulthood to be a period of increased specialization in this regard, and intellectual development to be adaptation to changing demands of work and social life. A persistent theme in the expertise literature is the central role attributed to domain-specific knowledge in expert performance. But what kind of knowledge constitutes expert knowledge? Is it explicit? Can it be taught? The proposition that expert knowledge is in part tacit knowledge is explored below.

Tacit Knowledge

It has been argued that expert performance in real-world settings relies to a degree on tacit knowledge, that is, knowledge that is usually not openly expressed or stated (Wagner and Sternberg, 1986). The last twenty years have seen increasing interest in the nature, role, and part played by tacit knowledge. A number of empirical and theoretical works have attempted to isolate what is distinctive about this particular form of knowledge. Much of the empirical work undertaken has been in real-world settings, and has found significant results on workplace performance in such diverse professions as academic psychology, management, computer programming, and welding. It is thus obvious that tacit knowledge is a measure of nonacademic ability that cannot be ignored. For adult educators, the fact that a significant portion of adult learning takes place at an implicit level has significant implications for the way programs are structured and presented.

It would seem that much professional knowledge is tacit. Sternberg and Caruso write, "One's ability to acquire tacit knowledge on the job will be a key factor in one's success or failure as a teacher. We suspect that failure to acquire sufficient tacit knowledge will result in rapid frustration and burnout" (1985, p. 148).

Earlier in their paper (p. 147), Sternberg and Caruso argued that most of the practical knowledge adults acquire is tacit, especially when it is learned on the job. Eraut (1985, p. 117) also sees tacit knowledge as part of professional knowledge. He groups tacit knowledge together with codified knowledge, which he understands as being embedded in traditions and craft procedures.

What follows is an outline of the theoretical underpinning of tacit knowledge, a review of the empirical results of several studies, and an analysis of the possible usefulness of tacit knowledge as a construct to explain superior workplace performance. We argue that tacit knowledge plays a largely unrecognized part in everyday life, supporting superior workplace skills and perhaps often providing the basis for expertise.

According to Broudy (1970, p. 83), the most ambitious claim to substantiate tacit knowledge as valid is found in the various works of Michael Polanyi. In *The Tacit Dimension* (1967), Polanyi asserts that as human beings "We know more than we can tell." He characterized the tacit as that which is implied, but not expressed in words, silent, unspoken. He commented, for example, that we can recognize a face without being able to specify its particulars. We do not remember a certain set of facial muscle positions, but we do know (tacitly) what emotion they express. (p. 12).

Polanyi distinguished between two terms of tacit knowing, the *proximal* (first or near) term and the *distal* (second or far) term. In the proximal term, we have knowledge we are unable to explicate. Broudy (1970) states that according to Polanyi, there are two kinds of knowing: the knowing of a thing by attending to it, the same way we attend to an entity as a whole; and the knowing of a thing by relying on our awareness of it for the purpose of attending to an entity to which it contributes, that is, tacit knowing.

In tacit knowing, meaning is separated from that which has meaning. Polanyi (p. 12) uses the example of a probe (a blind person's stick) to illustrate this. Anyone using a probe for the first time feels the impact against the palm or fingers. But as expertise increases, awareness of impact on the palm is transferred to a sense of the probe's point touching the objects explored. One becomes aware of the feelings in one's hands in terms of the meaning derived from the tip of the probe. Thus, the meaning of tacit knowing is displaced away from us, in this case, from the palm to the point of the probe.

Broudy (p. 101) describes a similar phenomenon in the aesthetic response to poetry: "A great deal of poetry written in English depends for its imagery on its Latin roots. . . . These Latin images function tacitly in the aesthetic response to poetry, and if the poet has these in mind, the reader who has a good dictionary meaning of the term, but not the appropriate image is simply not responding as the poet anticipated he would." That is, meaning is displaced from the concrete English meaning of the word to its Latin imagery.

This particular aspect of Polanyi's view on tacit knowledge may well have significance in enabling one to gain an understanding of expertise in practical areas such as hand-tool use, where tradespeople learn to "feel" with a tool, as an extension of themselves. An interesting example of this phenomenon is related by Evans and Butler (1992), who developed an expert model of welding that includes the following features:

1. Selection of the electrode and other aspects of preparation
2. Mutual planning and rehearsal of the actual welding process
3. Selecting position and posture so as to be able to maintain hand control
4. Observing and reacting to cues provided by the appearance of the weld pool, sound of the arc, and the feel of the arc
5. Interpreting the appearance of the weld

The authors saw the above as cues acting tacitly to guide expert welders. Item 4 especially relates closely to the phenomenon Polanyi described with probes. Evans and Butler found that expert welders processed a wide range of information to monitor the welding process—including the "feel" of the arc. Interestingly, the authors found that none of these expert cues, a definite feature of actual everyday welding practice, were mentioned anywhere in the various welding syllabi they examined. This suggests that perhaps the cues were in fact a tacit part of expert performance. For example, in twenty-eight trainee feedback sessions, only one welding instructor referred to the correct viscosity of the weld pool—signifying that many expert welders were not aware of (or perhaps simply chose not to teach) the necessary expert cues. This finding reflects the claim of Sternberg and Caruso (1985) that very little tacit knowledge is transferred via formal instruction; tacit knowledge is acquired through indirect instruction on the part of the self. It is "knowledge that, metaphorically, is acquired through osmosis" (p. 146). This they contrast to "Direct Learning," which is acquired from an immediate source such as a teacher, and "Mediated Learning," whereby stimuli from the environment are transformed by a mediation agent, usually a parent, sibling, or caregiver (p. 142).

The idea that much of our knowledge and learning is unavailable to us, being unconscious or implicit, is taken up by a number of other authors from very varied backgrounds. Norman (1988), for example, is concerned with the design of manufactured products. He notes that people are capable of "precise behavior from imprecise knowledge" (p. 56). He claims that much of the knowledge we need to function effectively does not need to be "in our heads" but can be "in the world." Much of the knowledge we need is "knowledge how," or to the psychologist, *procedural* as opposed to *declarative* knowledge—as such, it is "difficult or impossible to write down and difficult to teach. It is best taught by demonstration and best learned through practice. Even the best teachers cannot usually describe what they are doing" (pp. 57–58). Although not specifically referring to this kind of knowledge as tacit, he appears to be describing something very similar—if not identical.

Ehrlich and Soloway (1979) investigated tacit plan knowledge in computer programming. They attempted to tap into the specific tacit programming knowledge of expert and nonexpert computer programmers. They found that expert programmers used what the researchers called the "Running Total Loop Plan" when approaching new tasks, without being aware of using such a method. The results from their four studies were, they claimed, consistent with their predictions that tacit plan knowledge underlies the use of programming variables. Although they conceded their results could be interpreted differently, they claimed to have identified that the particular knowledge that expert programmers have over novices is tacit knowledge (p. 132).

Perhaps the most detailed investigation into tacit knowledge is the series of studies carried out by Wagner and Sternberg

(1986). They investigated the tacit knowledge possessed by two distinct groups of professionals: academic psychologists and business managers.

With the first group, they provided some 160 undergraduates, graduate students, and faculty members in psychology with a series of twelve everyday work-related situations, each with a number of possible answers. The experiment was repeated with the second cohort of 127 business subjects, who were also at undergraduate, graduate, and professional level. Their findings are as follows:

1. There were differences between experts and novices in tacit knowledge across groups whose members differed in amounts of experience and training in their respective fields.

2. There were strong relationships between performance on the tacit knowledge measure and various other measures of career performance, such as quality of faculty, number of papers published, prestige of company, and number of employees supervised.

3. Tacit knowledge scores of undergraduates were unrelated to their scores on a verbal ability test. (Other cohorts were not tested in verbal ability.)

Simosko (1991), is an acknowledged expert on the recognition or accreditation of prior learning. In her opinion, a great deal of what we have picked up during our lives is tacit, or in her word, unconscious: "As was pointed out . . . much of what we learn seems to be unconscious and many of the skills we possess are acquired seemingly accidentally" (p. 55).

Tacit knowledge has not escaped the attention of adult learning theorists either. Mezirow (1991a) refers to both tacit learning and tacit memory as integral parts of the adult learning process. (See also Andresen, 1991, p. 16, and Schön, 1983, 1987.)

The various empirical studies appear to indicate that tacit knowledge does play a part in workplace performance. According to a number of authors, it is one of the more significant differences between expert and novice performance. Understanding of the part played by tacit knowledge informs the debate on a range of issues, not the least of which concerns the structuring of teaching and learning environments. The problem for the adult educator is that an overemphasis on the tacit dimension of workplace skills may limit the definition of subject matter that can be taught, as expert performance comes to be understood as unteachable, implicit, or even elitist.

Implications for Adult Education

To date, there has been very little attempt to analyze the implications for adult education of the theory and research on practical intelligence, expertise, and tacit knowledge. However, to a large extent adult education is concerned with the enhancement of expertise. It is thus important for adult educators to know as much as possible about the nature and development of expertise, practical thinking, and implicit knowledge. Perhaps the most important issue centers on the relationship between educational program planning and notions of what constitutes expertise in a particular domain. Should the way experts operate dictate the nature of education and training programs? That is, should we simply mimic the processes underlying expert performance? Obviously, we need to have a notion of what constitutes expertise in a particular domain.

However, we also need to know something about the *development* of expertise. In all studies contrasting experts with novices, a consistent finding is that there is a distinct qualitative difference in the way they function. The implication is that this qualitative shift is an important feature in the acquisition of expertise. Clearly, one cannot be an expert without first being a novice. As adult educators, perhaps we should be as much concerned with teaching people to be novices as we are with teaching people to be experts. Having said this, it is equally important to know the process that makes the progression from novice to expert possible. At the core of this process is experience, but it is at this point that the literature on expertise begins to reveal some gaps. The question of the acquisition of expertise is not addressed sufficiently in the literature.

Instead of continuing to compare experts (much experience) with novices (little experience), it may be instructive to compare experts with nonexperts, nonexperts being those who do not seem to have profited from extensive experience. In this way we can begin to map the way in which experts, as opposed to nonexperts, utilize their experiences for learning.

It is crucial to distinguish between expertise as an outcome and the acquisition of expertise as a process. For example, in Chi, Glaser, and Farr's summary (1988) of the generic qualities of expertise, they note that experts are faster and more economical, partly because they do not conduct an extensive search of the available information. This does not imply that novices should be warned against conducting extensive searches of the data or urged to take shortcuts. Quite the contrary—extensive searches of the data are presumably important at the novice stage, and in this sense expertise is built upon the experience of being a novice. As adult educators, however, we are concerned with how experience is used to make someone an expert.

This leads to a second fundamental issue in connection with the literature on expertise. Is the process of becoming an expert generic or domain-specific? Does there exist a generic ability to learn from experience or is the process of learning from experience specific to a domain of knowledge and skill? Quite clearly, it is possible to identify generic aspects of learning from experience, and indeed the concept of "learning how to learn" has a special place in the adult education literature. However, the research on expertise cautions us against programs that attempt to teach people to learn how to learn as an end in itself, without reference to a domain of knowledge and skill. To be sure, it is important to understand generic aspects of the process of learning from experience, but any program designed to facilitate the development of expertise in a particular domain should take into account the way in which experts in that domain were able to use their experiences for learning.

Adult educators can take particular interest in the impact of general life experience on the development of expertise. Even though expertise is said to be domain-specific, many domains (for example, management) demand highly developed social and interpersonal skills that can be acquired through general life experience. In addition, general life experiences not only shape the perspectives or frames of reference one brings to the work environment, they can have an impact on specific aspects of practice (for example, pediatricians or child care workers experiencing parenthood, or marriage counselors marrying or divorcing). Research of this nature is still to be conducted.

Finally, the literature on expertise has implications for the way in which learning from prior experience is assessed. Schmidt, Norman, and Boshuizen (1990) refer to literature showing a decline in performance on certain measures of clinical reasoning among presumed medical experts (compared with recent graduates). This is because these measures are directed primarily at the novice stage of expertise (that is, an emphasis on all possible relevant knowledge in a particular presenting case), and fail to take into account the true nature of expertise. Assessment of prior experience, whether for entry to university study or for recertification of overseas qualifications, needs to be based on a clear idea of what expertise means in a given domain. In the case of entry to university, there are some further issues and problems relating to the curriculum and how this can best complement the expertise gained from prior experience (for example, successful managers enrolled in a business course, successful trainers enrolled in a course on human resource development, successful artists enrolled in a visual arts course). The findings of tacit knowledge research warn us, however, that people know more than they can tell. Howard (1988, p. 5) confirms this, finding that there is not necessarily any link between skill at explicit and implicit memory tasks. Thus assessment procedures and methods must not grant undue bias to those more fluent verbally, more reflective, and more able to argue their case than those perhaps equally skilled but less able to demonstrate their abilities in a test situation.

Conclusion

The literature on expertise, practical intelligence and thought, and tacit knowledge has great potential for informing and guiding adult education practice and for stimulating adult education research in its own right. It is important for adult educators to maintain a distinction between expertise as an outcome and the acquisition of expertise as a process. It is also important to understand and document how experts in particular domains have utilized their experience for learning. There is a need for research on how general life experience can have an impact on the development of expertise. And finally, assessments of the expertise gained from prior experience should be based on measures that recognize the true nature of expertise and its sometimes hidden nature.

Chapter Four

Theories of the Life Course

In the previous two chapters, we concentrated on the intellectual aspects of adult development: the growth or decline of adult intelligence, the nature of adult intelligence, and the results of some recent research on complementary cognitive constructs such as practical intelligence, tacit knowledge, and expertise. Thus, we have structured our argument to follow the traditional distinction between the development of adult cognitive functioning and the development of personality and social roles. The gap between the bodies of writings on these two aspects of development need not, however, be painted as broader than it is.

As discussed in Chapters Two and Three, it is now recognized that experience plays a key role in adult intellectual development, and especially in the development of expertise. The past understanding of intelligence as largely fixed and unalterable has given way. In its wake, the cognitive dimension of adulthood emerges as a complex and multifaceted combination of experience, wisdom, practical intelligence, tacit knowledge, and common sense. At the same time, developmental psychologists have been investigating the adult life course and the part played by normative and non-normative life events in shaping the core of what it is to be an adult. Here, as with intellectual development, experience—and the ability to reflect upon and learn from that experience—emerges as a key factor in the formation of adult personality and social roles.

The search for pattern, meaning, and purpose in life is an ancient and well-tried activity. Something of the spirit of this quest is captured in this passage from a historical novel about the Roman emperor Hadrian:

> The landscape of my days appears to be composed, like mountainous regions, of varied materials heaped up pell-mell. There I see my nature, itself composite, made up of equal parts of instinct and training. Here and there protrude the granite peaks of the inevitable, but all about is rubble from the landslips of chance. I strive to retrace my life to find in it some plan, following a vein of lead, or of gold, or the course of some subterranean stream, but such devices are only tricks of perspective in the memory. From time to time, in an encounter, or an omen, or in a particular series of happenings, I think that I recognize the working of fate, but too many paths lead nowhere at all, and too many sums add up to nothing. To be sure, I perceive in this diversity and disorder the presence of a person; but his form seems nearly always to be shaped by the pressure of circumstances; his features are blurred, like a figure reflected in water [Yourcenar, 1959, p. 26].

In this meditative passage, the emperor describes how he sees an underlying continuity in his identity, but feels it to be an identity without a strong profile, and one which appears subject to the vagaries of chance or circumstance. Casual observation confirms that this desire to make sense of one's biography is both powerful and widespread. What makes me the same person today as I was yesterday? Last year? Twenty or thirty years ago? Have I developed and changed? In what important ways do I differ from myself as a teenager? In what ways has my identity remained stable? Have any milestones or critical events shaped my life, or even transformed my identity? Or has my development been piecemeal and gradual, one phase of life merging imperceptibly into another? What have been the major influences in my life, the people and events that have shaped my beliefs, attitudes, and values? And how do I see the continuity between my past, present, and future self?

Questions such as these are not exclusively pertinent to individual biographies; they can also be found in various religious, literary, philosophical, and psychological texts that attempt to set out or discover patterns to the general life course. Most commonly, the life course is described in terms of a sequence of stages through which one progresses, at least ideally. For example, Aristotle proposed a three-stage model, Solon divided life into nine seven-year stages, Confucius identified six stages, The Sayings of the Fathers (from the Talmud) contain fourteen stages, and Shakespeare, of course, presented his well-known seven stages.

The psychological literature too contains propositions about the stages, tasks, or phases of life. Before considering this material, however, it is worthwhile addressing its relevance for the adult educator.

The identity of adult education as a field of study is largely premised on the identity of the adult. Much of the adult education literature, especially the literature on adult learning, makes reference to the distinct attributes of adults, and builds a rationale for practice based on these distinct attributes. For example, the greater experience of adults is already related to the adoption of experiential and group techniques, and the purported desire for autonomy and self-direction among adults is related to the adoption of negotiated learning and learning contracts. Because adult education necessarily involves some kind of intervention in the lives of participants, it is important for adult educators to recognize the nature and limits of this intervention, and to locate their intervention in some kind of life-span framework.

Many adult education programs are explicitly designed to promote personal change or development, and are geared towards addressing life-span concerns such as gender roles, marriage, divorce, retirement, parenting, racial discrimination, health, sexuality, spiritual growth, unemployment, migration, and so on. Adult educators who wish to promote transformation need to develop an understanding of the processes of transformation, and different developmental theories offer different interpretations of the nature of transformation. In addition, adult educators have an interest in promoting the idea of lifelong learning and the notion of the lifelong learner. The ideal lifelong learner is often portrayed as having self-knowledge, self-worth, a sense of autonomy, and a desire to fulfill personal potential. Thus the development of the lifelong learner can be located within a broader view of adult development.

Stages and Phases of Development

This chapter reviews a number of frequently cited stage, phase, and task models of adult development. Each of these models presents a descriptive account of development, an explanation of the fundamental processes underlying developmental progress, and a clear view of the end point of development: the mature, fully developed, psychologically healthy person. Our interest in these early works is that, collectively, they provide different ways of looking at the relationship between self and other during the life course, the role of experience in development, and the importance of autonomy as a developmental concept. Each theory will be looked at in terms of these three aspects.

Levinson (1978) focused on the decade between the ages of thirty-five and forty-five. He believed that during this decade one made the shift from youth to middle age. Because he wanted to study each of his subjects intensively and examine their lives in detail, he decided on a small sample, forty individuals. He chose to study only men, partly because he acknowledged the difference between men and women and partly because he was interested in his own psychological development as a male. He divided his sample into four occupational subgroups to represent diverse sections of society and to explore his belief that work is of central psychological importance for the self. The four groups comprised ten hourly workers from two companies, ten executives from two companies, ten academic biologists from two universities, and ten novelists who had published at least two books. The sample included people from diverse social classes, racial/ethnic/religious origins, and levels of educational attainment. Levinson describes his research method as follows: "A biographical interview combines aspects of a research interview, a clinical interview and a conversation between friends. . . . Our essential method was to elicit the life stories of forty men, to construct biographies and to develop generalizations based upon these biographies. . . . In each case we began by immersing ourselves in the interview material and working toward an intuitive understanding of the man and his life. Gradually we tried more interpretive formulations and, going back and forth between the interviews and the analysis, came to a construction of the life course" (pp. 15–16).

Following the interviews, it became apparent to Levinson that he was investigating not only the chosen decade, but, retrospectively, the earlier years of the lives of these men. He therefore expanded the scope of his theorizing to include the period from entry into adulthood until the late forties.

The descriptive part of Levinson's theory is simple to state. The life cycle comprises a sequence of four eras, each lasting for approximately twenty-five years. He also identifies a number of developmental periods within these eras, concentrating on early and middle adulthood. Here are the eras and main developmental periods he identifies:

1. Childhood and adolescence: birth to age twenty (early childhood transition by age three)
2. Early adulthood: age seventeen to forty-five
   Early adult transition—seventeen to twenty-two
   Entering the adult world—twenty-two to twenty-eight
   Age thirty transition—twenty-eight to thirty-three
   Settling down—thirty-three to forty
3. Middle adulthood: age forty to sixty-five
   Midlife transition—forty to forty-five
   Entering middle adulthood—forty-five to fifty
   Age fifty transition—fifty to fifty-five
   Culmination of middle adulthood—fifty-five to sixty

4. Late adulthood: age sixty on

Late adult transition—sixty to sixty-five

According to Levinson, each era has its distinct and unifying character of living. Each transition between eras thus requires a basic change in the character of one's life, which may take between three and six years to complete. Within the broad eras are periods of development, each period being characterized by a set of tasks and an attempt to build or modify one's life structure. For example, in the Early Adult Transition period the two primary tasks are to move out of the preadult world and to make a preliminary step into the adult world. Similarly, during the Settling Down period, the two tasks are to establish a niche in society and to work for progress and advancement in that niche. A pervasive theme throughout the various periods is the existence of the "Dream." It has the quality of a vision, an imagined possibility that generates excitement and vitality. It is our projection of the ideal life. The place and nature of the "Dream" in one's life is constantly modified and revisited throughout the life course as the imagined self is compared with the world as it is lived.

Another fundamental process occurring throughout the life cycle is that of individuation. This refers to the changing relationship between self and the external world throughout the life course. It begins with the infant's dawning knowledge of its separate existence in a world of animate and inanimate objects. It is apparent in the tasks of the Early Adult Transition; one of the principal tasks being to modify or terminate existing relationships with family and significant others and to reappraise and modify the self accordingly. Indeed, much of developmental progress is couched in terms of the changing nature of the relationship between self and others, such as mentor relationships, love and family relationships, and occupational relationships. In Midlife, relationships are reappraised again; this takes the form of a struggle between the polarities of attachment and separateness:

We use the term "attachment" in the broadest sense, in order to encompass all the forces that connect person and environment. To be attached is to be engaged, involved, needy, plugged in, seeking, rooted. . . .

At the opposite pole is separateness. This is not the same thing as isolation or aloneness. A person is separate when he is primarily involved in his inner world—a world of imagination, fantasy, play. His main interest is not in adapting to the "real world" but in constructing and exploring an imagined world, the enclosed world of his inner self [p. 239].

Levinson views Midlife as a period where one needs to redress the dominance of attachment to the external world: to find a better balance between the needs of the self and the needs of society—a greater integration of separateness and attachment: "Greater individuation allows him to be more separate from the world, to be more independent and self generating. But it also gives him the confidence and understanding to have more intense attachments in the world and to feel more fully a part of it" (p. 195).

Individuation is also apparent in the attempt to integrate polarities within the self, such as the masculine and feminine polarity, and the polarities between young and old, destruction and creation. The process of individuation is thus paradoxical: it points to a developmental move away from the world, but this independence and separateness is used to make the individual part of the world and to integrate previously separated aspects of the self.

It is true that Levinson's theory was based on a male-only sample and that he did not intend it to be applied to the experiences of women. Nevertheless, it has been quite widely popularized, often without the caveat that it applies only to men. It has helped to shape the discourse on the nature of adult development, irrespective of gender. For these reasons, a number of subsequent studies have attempted to evaluate the applicability of the theory to the experiences of women. Before discussing them, it is worthwhile noting the position of Gilligan (1986), a pioneer critic of the gender bias evident in developmental theory in general. She argues that terms like separateness, autonomy, and independence are essentially male values and that females value relationships and responsibilities, empathy and attachment, and interdependence rather than independence. While the identity of boys is built upon contrast and separateness from their primary caregiver (who in most instances is female), the identity of girls is built on the perception of sameness and attachment to their primary caregiver:

> Consequently, relationships, and particularly issues of dependency, are experienced differently by women and men. For boys and men, separation and individuation are critically tied to gender identity since separation from the mother is essential for the development of masculinity. For girls and women, issues of femininity or feminine identity do not depend on the achievement of separation from the mother or on the progress of individuation. Since masculinity is defined through separation while femininity is defined through attachment, male gender identity is threatened by intimacy, while female gender identity is threatened by separation. Thus males tend to have difficulty with relationships, while females tend to have problems with individuation. The quality of embeddedness in social interaction and personal relationships that characterizes women's lives in contrast to men's, however, becomes not only a descriptive difference but also a developmental liability when the milestones of childhood and adolescent development in the psychological literature are markers of increasing separation. Women's failure to separate then becomes by definition a failure to develop [1986, pp. 8–9].

Gilligan's argument is that womanhood is rarely equated with mature healthy adulthood in much of the developmental literature. This is because the idea of the healthy, developed personality is predominantly portrayed from a male perspective.

What then have been the results of those studies which have explicitly aimed to validate or test Levinson's model using female subjects? Caffarella and Olson (1993) have documented nine such studies, the results of which are summarized in Table 4.1.

These research studies typically employed the intensive interview technique. The results are rather mixed: in many cases the developmental periods described by Levinson were in fact useful as a framework for making sense of the experiences of the women studied. However, there were significant differences among the women; for example, very few described a "Dream" in which career accomplishment played a major role. Some studies found that the developmental tasks occurred within a different time frame (for example, women resuming their undergraduate education in their thirties and forties), or that there was greater variety in the balance of family and career commitments. Other studies did not find Levinson's developmental periods applicable to an all-female sample.

Caffarella and Olson (1993) also review a group of studies seeking to document the life cycle of women in their own right. The results support the view expressed by Gilligan that women, in contrast to men, place a high value on relationships and interdependence. A summary of the results appears in Table 4.2.

Caffarella and Olson identify four major themes in the studies they reviewed. In general, the studies found that interpersonal relationships are extremely important to women's self-concept. The women in the studies recognized the importance of taking a role but had difficulty balancing the roles their lives offered (mother, wife, paid employee). Rather than a single series of stages, the women's development tended to be diverse and nonlinear, with significant discontinuities introduced by changes in role. This diversity was further heightened by the developmental expectations of different cohorts, with younger women looking to types of role models that were not available to middle-aged or older women at a similar point in their lives. Nonetheless, despite the multiplicity of patterns and the need to "maintain a 'fluid' sense of self," Cafarella and Olson conclude, "The importance of relationships and a sense of connectedness to others was . . . central to the overall developmental process throughout a woman's life span" (1993, p. 143).

Table 4.1. Tests of Levinson's Model on Female Subjects.

Author(s)	Subjects	Data Collection Techniques	Selected Salient Results
Alexander, K. (1980)	N = 37; Age 19–36 SES = predominantly middle class EI = Caucasian Enrolled in college	Author designed, semistructured interview Author-designed life satisfaction/ dissatisfaction graph	Women studied did experience stages that Levinson found for men, but the issues within those stages were different. The age 30 transition included an acceptance of responsibility for self.
Barner, A. (1981)	N = 134; Age 27–53 SES = not specified EI = not specified Enrolled in community college	Tennessee Self-Concept Scale (TSCS) Author-designed descriptive questionnaire	Those women in the stable periods (defined as Levinson's model) had higher self-esteem than those in transition periods. Respondents in the youngest age group (age 27–32) reported the greatest amount of questioning and self-doubt.
Goodman, S. (1980)	N = 30; Age 45–60 SES = predominantly middle class EI = Caucasian	Modification of Alexander (1980) interview guide	Levinson's notice of life structures were confirmed by this study, though only a few of the women experienced the midlife transition described by the men in Levinson's study. The focus of the lives of the majority of these women was on marriage and childbearing.

Table 4.1. Tests of Levinson's Model on Female Subjects, Cont'd.

Author(s)	Subjects	Data Collection Techniques	Selected Salient Results
Jeffries, D. L. (1985)	N = 40; Age 20–40 SES = appears middle and lower class EI = Black	Biographical interviewing using author-designed structured interview (Jeffries-Winbush Black Lifespan Assessment Question-naire)	No correlation was found between age and the prescribed development tasks. Unique stages and characteristics exist that are culture-specific in nature and typically relate to black female devel-opment.
Kahnweiler, J. (1980)	N = 40; Age 30–50 SES = middle class EI = Caucasian Enrolled in college	Author-designed questionnaire	Respondents were focused on their own personal goals for the future. They felt a real time limitation as they were just get-ting to the point of forming a "dream" for their lives.
Murrell, H. and Donahue, W. (1982)	N = 44; Age 34–65 SES = upper middle class EI = not specified Senior-level college administrators	Modification of Levinson (1977) inter-view guide	These women reported age-related transi-tional periods in their lives (for example, in the 30s, if career ori-ented shift to family orientation and vice versa; in 40s an iden-tity crisis)
Roberts, P. and Newton, P. M. (1987)	*N = 39; Age 28–53 SES = unknown	Biographical interview based on modifications of the	Suggest underlying pat-tern of women's development with age linked stable and transitional periods.

Table 4.1. Tests of Levinson's Model on Female Subjects, Cont'd.

Author(s)	Subjects	Data Collection Techniques	Selected Salient Results
	EI = Predominantly Caucasian, with 8 black subjects	Levinson instrument	The age 30 transition was especially consistent for these respondents. As women's dreams of their adult life were more complex than most men's (involving marriage, motherhood and career), their life structures seemed less stable and more conflicted. The relational aspect was seen as key in shaping the lives of these women.
Stewart, W. (1977)	N = 11; Age 31–39 SES = predominantly middle class EI = Caucasian	Author-designed, semistructured interview based on Levinson's "Guidelines for Interviews"	These women demonstrated greater variability than men in the accomplishment of certain developmental tasks, and this variability appeared to be related to whether the woman marries or remains single and/or pursues a career. The life "dreams" form tended to have a strong relational component.
Zubrod, L. (1980)	N = 30; Age 32–44 SES = all social strata	Modification of Alexander (1980) interview guide	The broad outlines of the developmental periods of early adulthood (17–40) were

Table 4.1. Tests of Levinson's Model on Female Subjects, Cont'd.

Author(s)	Subjects	Data Collection Techniques	Selected Salient Results
	represented EI = Caucasian Included people from one urban and one rural community	Lifeline Chart	generally the same for women as for the men in Levinson's study. The nature and time of the developmental tasks were different than was noted for the men in the Levinson study. The central issue of the age 30 transition was the separation/individualization process, while the major pull at age 35 was to do something significant.

Note: SES = Socioeconomic Status
 EI   = Ethnic Identity

*Combination of 4 earlier studies.

Source: selected from Caffarella and Olson, 1993, pp 129–132; reproduced with permission.

This research on women's development highlights one of the limitations of Levinson's theory, that it does not adequately represent the experiences of social groups such as women, blacks, indigenous populations, migrants, and those living in poverty. This limitation is arguably a feature of much of the developmental literature. For example, Chickering and Havighurst (1981) describe a number of developmental tasks that typify the life course in white, middle-class North American culture. The tasks include "achieving emotional independence" in late adolescence and youth, "deciding on a partner" in early adulthood, "revising career plans" at the midlife transition, "making mature civic contributions" in

Table 4.2. Studies Documenting the Life Cycle of Women.

Author(s)	Subjects	Data Collection Techniques	Selected Salient Results
Baruch, G., Barnett, R. and Rivers, C. (1983)	Phase I: N = 60; Age 35–55 SES = lower class to middle class EI = Caucasian Phase II: N = 238; Age 35–55 SES = lower class to upper middle class	Phase I— Author-designed, unstructured interviews Phase II— Author designed in-terview, and standardized measures in-corporated in-to the survey	A two-dimensional pic-ture of well-being was formulated, that of mastery (the doing side of life) and plea-sure (the feeling side). In general it was hypothesized that women's well-being is linked more to social climate than internal changes.
Bateson, M. C. (1989)	N = 5 Age = not specified SES = middle and upper middle EI = not given	Author-designed in-depth open-ended inter-views	Fluidity and disconti-nuity are hallmarks of women's lives. Major chasm appeared between earlier socialization and mature adult roles. Growth came from col-legiality, friendships, and relationships with significant others. Caring (for others and self) crosses all spheres of women's lives. A central survival skill is the capacity to pay attention to and respond to changing circumstances and to live with ambiguity.

Table 4.2. Studies Documenting the Life Cycle of Women, Cont'd.

Author(s)	Subjects	Data Collection Techniques	Selected Salient Results
Gilligan, C. (1977, 1982)	N=21; Age 15–33 SES = diverse EI = diverse	Author-designed, semistruc-tured inter-view	Women's moral judg-ments proceed through three levels: focus on self (level one), to the concept of responsibility for self and others with the good equated with caring for others (level two), to the subsuming of both conventions (caring for others as equated with good) and indi-vidual needs under the moral principle of nonviolence (level three).
			Within this process of making moral judg-ments, two important transitions are made: the movement from selfishness to respon-sibility and a second from goodness to truth.
Hancock, E. (1981, 1985)	N = 20; Age 30–75 SES = diverse, but primarily well-educated middle class EI = not given	Author-designed, semistruc-tured inter-view	Adulthood for these women was anchored in their choices and need for self and direction in the con-text of relationships and care.
			These women tended to alternate patterns

Table 4.2. Studies Documenting the Life Cycle of Women, Cont'd.

Author(s)	Subjects	Data Collection Techniques	Selected Salient Results
			of work and family, but for those who combined both, relationship was the central focus.
			Life phases for these women were defined by the changes in their social commitments (for example, marriage, children, divorce), rather than by age or occupation.
			Female identity development is given a circular shape versus a linear pattern and is viewed as organic and dynamic.
			Women as adults rediscover "the girl within" to retrieve an original sense of self. A blending of values of cooperation, care, and competence are viewed as key to women's development.
McLean, P. (1980)	N=502; Age 25–50 SES = predominantly middle class EI = not given	Author-designed questionnaire Bradburn's Overall Happiness Scale	These women portrayed a complex life pattern, with a constant shift in roles throughout their lives.

Table 4.2. Studies Documenting the Life Cycle of Women, Cont'd.

Author(s)	Subjects	Data Collection Techniques	Selected Salient Results
		Gough's Adjective Checklist	Substantial discontinuity was found in the importance these women attached to various roles, particularly the work and family roles.
Reinke, B. J., Holmes, D. S. and Harris, R. L. (1985)	N = 60; Age 35–45 SES = middle class EI = 58 Caucasian, 2 minority	Author-designed questionnaire structured interview focused on social history and inner subjectivity perspective	Women's lives displayed immense diversity in terms of psychosocial changes.

Transitions in these women's lives were found to be related to chronological age as well as role-related changes.

A major transition in their lives was manifested between the ages 27 and 30 and was characterized by personal disruption, reassessment and finally, an increased sense of well-being. This transition was not related to family cycle phase. |
| Rubin, E. (1979) | N = 150; Age 34–54 SES = working, middle class El = Caucasian | Author-designed, semi-structured interview | These women when describing themselves usually spoke in terms of "being" versus doing. This held true even for those |

Table 4.2. Studies Documenting the Life Cycle of Women, Cont'd.

Author(s)	Subjects	Data Collection Techniques	Selected Salient Results
			women who worked outside the home.
			Almost all of these women exhibited a decided sense of relief at the departure of their children, versus seeing that as a difficult transition. Rather the difficulty stemmed from the fact that they were facing a new beginning in their lives.
			The idea of the elusive self, the "who am I," was evidenced by many of these women.

Note: SES = Socioeconomic Status
    EI   = Ethnic Identity

Source: Caffarella and Olsen, 1993, pp. 129–132, reproduced with permission.

middle adulthood, and "adjusting to retirement" in late adulthood. These tasks read like a socially approved timetable for individual growth and development. Indeed, this is precisely how they are conceived; note Havighurst's comments on his original inventory: "The tasks the individual must learn—the developmental tasks of life— are those things that constitute health and satisfactory growth in our society. They are the things a person must learn if he is to be judged and to judge himself to be a reasonably happy and successful person. A developmental task is a task which arises at or about a certain period in the life of the individual, successful achievement of which leads to his happiness and to success with later tasks, while failure leads to unhappiness in the individual, disapproval by society, and difficulty with later tasks" (1972, p. 2).

Havighurst offers no vision for development beyond complete capitulation to the expectations of society: the particular social and historical circumstances in which the individual is located are simply taken as given. This of course highlights a core problem for developmental psychologists: how best to conceive the relationship between individual psychological development and the demands and expectations of society. To what extent is satisfactory development predicated on social approval or at least harmony between individual and social needs?

Most developmental psychologists portray development, in part, as a strengthening of the self in relation to the power of social forces. For example, Levinson uses the revealing term "self-generating" to describe his concept of individuation. What is implied here is the idea that social influences on the formation of identity become weakened with developmental progress. That is, we become relatively liberated from the sociocultural constraints that shape our identity, a process Levinson refers to as "detribalization." Although Levinson acknowledges the dialectical interplay of self and world, he ultimately views the test of developmental progress as the ascendancy of the self, its ability to stand apart and separate from the world.

This concept of autonomy is expressed in a variety of ways in different theories. In Maslow (1968), it is found in the construct of "self-actualization." In his words, once we have achieved a certain level of maturity, we "are motivated primarily by trends to self-actualization (defined as on-going actualization of potentials, capacities and talents, as fulfillment of a mission)." The qualities of self-actualized people are

They are realistic.

They accept themselves, other people, and the natural world for what they are.

They have a great deal of spontaneity.

They are problem-centered rather than self-centered.

They have an air of detachment and a need for privacy.

They are autonomous and independent.

Their appreciation of people and things is fresh rather than stereotyped.

Most of them have had profound mystical or spiritual experiences, although not necessarily religious in character.

They identify with humanity.

Their intimate relationships with a few specially loved people tend to be profound and deeply emotional rather than superficial.

Their values and attitudes are democratic.

They do not confuse means with ends.

Their sense of humor is philosophical rather than hostile.

They have a great fund of creativity.

They resist conformity to the culture.

They transcend the environment rather than just cope with it.

The paradoxical quality of being separate while being more attached is clearly apparent in Maslow's description of the self-actualized person, as is the capacity of the self to transcend the world. Words like *privacy*, *autonomous*, *detached*, *transcend*, and *independent* are used alongside phrases like "profound intimate relationships," "deeply emotional," and "identify with humanity."

For Gould (1978), adult development is based on our ability to separate ourselves from the false assumptions of childhood:

By striving for a fuller, more independent adult consciousness, we trigger the angry demons of childhood consciousness. Growing and reformulating our self-definition becomes a dangerous act. It is the act of transformation.

Adult consciousness progresses between ages 16 and 50 by our mastering childhood fear, by learning to leash and modulate the childhood anger released by change. As we strive to live up to our full adult potential, we confront layer after layer of buried childhood pain. Adult consciousness then, evolves through a series of confrontations with our own primitive past. Finally, as adults we can begin to master demonic reality and rework the irrationalities of childhood [p. 25].

Gould outlines the major false assumptions about ourselves that prevent us from being truly adult. We develop adult consciousness by shedding these assumptions. He distinguishes periods in development in terms of the false assumptions which characterize the period. For example the major false assumption of the period "Leaving our parent's world" (sixteen to twenty-two years of age) is "I'll always belong to my parents and believe in their world." This assumption, like all the assumptions described, is a protective device which on the one hand is a source of comfort and security to the youth who is becoming independent, but on the other hand constitutes a limit on independence. From these early first steps toward independence, there is a continual struggle with childhood false assumptions until "the life of inner directedness finally prevails" at the close of midlife. Gould remarks: "we make the final passage from 'I am theirs' to 'I own myself'" (p. 310). Thus the self is able to transcend the world, so to speak, through transcending the false assumptions of childhood.

In the developmental stages proposed by Loevinger (1976), the theme of separation is all-pervading. In the earliest stages, the presocial and the symbiotic, the primary task is to differentiate self from nonself and to consolidate the sense of being a separate person. The impulsive stage is characterized by the attempt to impose the self on the world: because this naturally meets with resistance (often in the form of punishment), the child eventually learns some degree of self-control. This self-control is rather instrumental, designed to pursue impulses while protecting the self from punishment (hence the name: Self-Protective stage). The Conformist stage occurs when the child starts to identify his or her own interests with that of the group. The child is a conformist and, at least on the surface, values niceness, helpfulness, and cooperation with others. At this point, we can see that self-identity is very much tied to social rules and regulations, but it is a rather blind conformism, without much sense of self-awareness. During the Self-Aware and Conscientious stages which follow, the child is more conscious of an inner life or self and that others have inner lives. With this awareness comes a sense of moral responsibility: "Along with the concepts of responsibility and obligations go the correlative concepts of privileges, rights, and fairness. All of them imply a sense of choice rather than being a pawn of fate. The Conscientious person sees himself (herself) as the origin of his (her) own destiny" (p. 21). The following stages: Individualistic, Autonomous, and Integrated, begin with a heightened sense of individuality, one where inner conflicts and emotional dependence are recognized. During the Autonomous stage, the person finally accepts the inevitability of inner conflict and the conflict between needs and duties. There is also an acceptance of the limitations of autonomy and the inevitability of emotional interdependence. The Integrated stage brings with it a certain transcending of the conflicts apparent in the Autonomous stage; Loevinger refers to it as being similar to the concept of self-actualization. It is interesting that Loevinger refers to autonomy as having a component of interdependence—indeed she distinguishes the Individualistic from the Autonomous stage, defining the latter as a stage of development that goes beyond individualism.

Erikson (1959) is another developmental theorist who recognizes that a strong sense of identity leads naturally to a capacity for interdependence. He describes a sequence of eight "psychosocial stages." The first five stages comprise childhood and are basically an expansion of Freud's view of psychosexual development, but with an explicit recognition of social influences. Erikson's view is that development occurs as the ego adjusts to meet the changing demands of society. These demands promote a struggle or crisis within the person, and it is this struggle that defines a particular stage. The emotional crises, the values emerging from them, and the corresponding period of life (or "stage") are shown in Table 4.3.

When Erikson speaks of the first social achievement of the infant as "the willingness to let the mother out of sight without undue anxiety or rage, because she has become an inner certainty as well as an outer predictability," he is referring to the conflict between basic trust versus mistrust. He goes on to explain that the state of trust "implies not only that one has learned to rely on the sameness and continuity of the outer providers, but also that one may trust oneself and the capacity of one's own organs to cope with urges" (1959, p. 61). This is the first stage in developing a sense of identity: to trust the other and thereby trust oneself. In young adulthood the crisis of intimacy versus isolation illustrates quite nicely how intimacy (read "interdependence") is predicated on a strong sense of personal identity. Intimacy is described by Erikson as a fusion of one's identity with that of others. If one avoids the experience of intimacy because of a fear of losing one's ego, then isolation and self-absorption will be the outcome. In Erikson's theory, then, once the identity crisis of adolescence has been addressed, further developmental progress focuses on the relationship with the other rather than with the self. This is also true of the adulthood stage, where there is a concern with establishing and guiding the next generation, and the maturity stage, where the sense of ego integrity as opposed to despair is cast very much in terms of the capacity to both accept oneself and simultaneously transcend oneself and see one's personal life in its broader historical and cultural context.

Alternatives to Stage and Phase Theories

All the above approaches attempt to chart the life course in terms of a sequence of phases or stages: periods of stability, equilibrium, and balance that alternate, in a largely predictable way, with periods of instability and transition. However, there has always been an

Table 4.3. Stages of Human Life.

Opposing issues of each stage	Significant relations	Psychosocial modalities
1. Basic trust versus mistrust (approx. 1 year)	Maternal person	To get To give in return
2. Autonomy versus shame and doubt (2–3 years)	Parental persons	To hold on To let go
3. Initiative versus guilt (4–5 years)	Basic family	To make ("going after") To make like ("playing")
4. Industry versus inferiority (6–11 years)	"Neighborhood," school	To complete things To make things together
5. Identity versus identity (role) confusion (12–18 years)	Peer group, outgroups, leadership models	To be oneself (or not) To share being oneself
6. Intimacy versus isolation (18–35 years)	Partners in friendship, sex, competition, cooperation	To lose and find oneself in another
7. Generativity versus stagnation (self-absorption) (35–60 years)	Divided labor and shared household	To make be To take care of
8. Integrity versus despair (and disgust) (60+ years)	"Mankind," "my kind"	To be, through having been To face not being

Source: Based on Erikson (1959).

opposing view within psychology, pointing to the huge individual variability in the way the life course is constructed.

Neugarten (1976) made an explicit distinction between social time, historical time, and life time (that is, chronological age), in charting the course of the life cycle. With respect to social time, she observes:

> Every society is age-graded, and every society has a system of social expectations regarding age-appropriate behavior. The individual passes through a socially regulated cycle from birth to death as inexorably as he passes through the biological cycle: a succession of socially delineated age-statuses, each with its recognized rights, duties, and obligations. There exists a socially prescribed timetable for the ordering of major life events: a time in the lifespan when men and women are expected to marry, a time to raise children, a time to retire. This normative pattern is largely adhered to, more or less consistently, by most persons within a given social group [p. 16].

Neugarten goes on to note that the social change associated with historical time leads to a change in age norms and in expectations regarding age-appropriate behavior. In addition to social and historical time, there are changes that are age-related and arise more from within the individual than from without. These internal changes are forged through our experiences and our growing capacity to interpret experience in a more encompassing and refined way. However, social time takes the leading role in Neugarten's analysis. She argues that so-called life crises, such as the empty nest, menopause, and retirement are not really experienced as crises if they occur on time, as part of the expected life cycle. It is the unexpected life events, or those expected events that occur "off-time," that are the potential crises. Thus, although Neugarten acknowledges that the life cycle is ordered, she views it as largely a social ordering, and asserts that there is no necessary order to the crises we experience in our development. This is because a life crisis is defined in terms of incongruity between our experience and our expectations. Development, then, cannot be conceived in terms of an orderly sequence of life crises, as some theorists have proposed.

Baltes and his colleagues (Baltes, Cornelius, and Nesselroade, 1980; Baltes, Reese, and Lipsitt, 1980) make similar distinctions to those of Neugarten. They argue that developmental processes may begin at any point in life and are not necessarily linear (that is, a developmental theme, such as dependence, may be more salient in early and late life than it is in middle life). They recognize three influences on development which together account for substantial individual variation. First, there are normative age-graded influences: those correlated highly with age, such as physical maturation, commencement of education, and parents' death. Then, there are normative, history-graded influences, that is, historical events that influence entire age cohorts—economic depressions, epidemics, wars, social movements. Finally, there are a host of nonnormative influences: events that have great impact on individual lives but that most people escape, such as contracting a rare disease, having a child with a genetic abnormality, or winning a lottery. Baltes, Reese, and Lipsitt (1980) summarize these three influences in terms of whether they are primarily age-related (that is, related to a person's own life span) or cohort-specific (that is, related to the point in history when a person was born).

- *Normative Age-Graded:* Biological and sociocultural influences that are linked fairly clearly with age, such as physical maturation during childhood or typical events during adulthood involving the family, education, and occupation.

- *Normative History-Graded:* Environmental, cataclysmic, and social influences that affect most members of a culture at the same time, like wars, sweeping economic or technological changes, and major epidemics. These effects may differ depending on a person's age at the time of the event, but most people of a given age—a whole cohort—will have similar experiences.

- *Nonnormative:* Events that are significant for a particular individual, but are not part of an overall pattern tied to the life cycle, like traffic accidents, lottery winnings, and religious conversion.

With two of the three major influences on development relatively unrelated to age, the attempt to identify universal age-related stages or phases seems bound to fail.

Riegel (1976) was one of the earlier writers to make this point when he argued for a dialectical understanding of human development. In his view, there is a constant dialectic between the developing person and the evolving society. The individual is considered a changing person in a changing world. Human development is conceived as moving along at least four dimensions:

1. The inner-biological dimension—maturation, health
2. The individual-psychological dimension—self-concept, self-esteem, ideal self
3. The cultural-sociological dimension—social organization, rules, regulations, rituals
4. The outer physical dimension—natural catastrophe, economic conditions

In this scenario, stable periods of equilibrium and balance are the exception rather than the rule. When any two of the dimensions are in conflict, a crisis with the potential to generate developmental change may occur. For example:

Inner-biological progressions lead the individual away from home, to work, marriage, and parenthood. Most of these events will be well synchronized with progressions along other dimensions. For example, many individuals marry when they are mature enough, when they have the appropriate psychological stature and intention, and when the social conditions are conducive and appropriate. In other instances synchronization is not achieved. Individuals marry without having reached a sufficient level of maturity; others have attained the proper level but fail to find the right partner. Thus the inner-biological and individual-psychological progressions are not always synchronized with the cultural-sociological and outer physical conditions [Riegel, 1976, pp. 693–694].

The point is that synchronization is rare, and development is therefore a continuing process of change: "Plateaus of balance, stability, and equilibrium occur when the developmental or historical task is completed. But developmental and historical tasks are never completed. At the very moment when completion seems to be achieved, new questions and doubts arise in the individual and in society. The organism, the individual, society, and even outer nature are never at rest, and in their restlessness they are rarely in perfect harmony" (p. 697).

Perhaps, as educators, we should avoid any preconceived notions about predictable and relatively stable stages or phases of development, and should focus more on the process of change and transformation and the ways the various influences on development interact. Perhaps, also, we should abandon notions of an ideal end point to development. This seems to be the direction taken by two adult educators, Merriam and Clark, in their study *Lifelines: Patterns of Work, Love, and Learning in Adulthood* (1991). Their focus on work and love was inspired by Freud's reported answer to a question concerning what a normal person should be able to do well; he replied "Lieben und arbeiten," to love and to work. Their study assumes that love and work are two central social and psychological forces in adult life and that learning has a role to play in the life events surrounding these two dimensions of adulthood. They used a questionnaire where love and work events over a period of twenty years were rated as good, bad, or OK. Significant learning events over the same period were also documented. The questionnaire was distributed to graduate and continuing education course participants, adults in community organizations, cooperative extension workers, and church groups. There were 410 usable responses. In addition, nineteen interviews were conducted where participants discussed and further elaborated on their questionnaire responses. They found three patterns of work and love over the period studied:

1. The divergent pattern, where if one domain is rated as good the other domain is rated low.
2. The steady/fluctuating pattern, where one domain remains steady while the other fluctuates.
3. The parallel pattern, where work and love events are evaluated as moving together (that is, when one is rated as good in a particular year the other is also rated as good).

Examples of these three patterns are shown in Figure 4.1.

Significantly, these patterns were not related to periods in adult life, defined as young adulthood, (that is, the twenties), the thirties (through age forty), and middle age (forty-one through sixty-two). Furthermore, the patterns were stable over the time period studied, and they were not related to gender. Merriam and Clark, then, using the basic dimensions of love and work, illustrate how different basic patterns can emerge and remain stable across the life span. However, development occurs within these patterns through significant learning experiences associated with life events. Development occurs through expanding skills and abilities, sense of self, and life perspective, and sometimes through a transformation of the whole person.

Merriam and Clark present a view of the nature of development underlying the patterns of work and love, but it is a pluralistic conception. For example, when they illustrate how the sense of self can expand, they offer two possibilities: "The dimension we are calling sense of self relates to the impact of learning on the person's identity. The sense of self is expanded in two ways: either through development of greater independence and autonomy, or through the establishment of an increased sense of relatedness or connection" (p. 205).

Figure 4.1. Patterns of Work and Love.

The Divergent Pattern

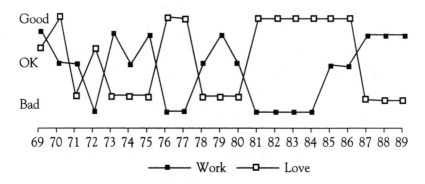

The Steady/Fluctuating Pattern

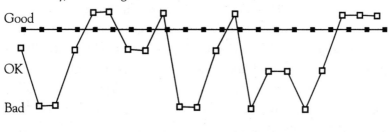

The Parallel Pattern

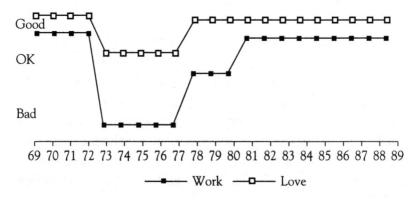

Source: Merriam and Clark, 1991, pp. 75, 100, 129. Reproduced with permission.

Merriam and Clark offer an alternative to the concept of development as a linear and single pathway, driven by a unitary process (such as the challenging of childhood assumptions). Instead, they see development as a product of the learning associated with significant life events, and this learning typically leads to multiple and nonlinear pathways. For them, the issue is how we learn from life experiences rather than how life experiences constrain or limit our learning.

Conclusion

There is a growing recognition within psychology that development needs to be understood, not only in terms of normative age-graded stages but also in terms of nonnormative life events. The influence of historical events and social movements is also acknowledged, so that development is conceived as following complex patterns that differ between individuals, rather than as a simple linear progression through a relatively fixed sequence of stages toward a common goal.

The task then becomes to understand how development, in whatever form it takes, is triggered and sustained: What kinds of processes lead to developmental growth? This question demands more than a psychological answer—even the psychological literature acknowledges the importance of historical, social, and cultural influences on development. Indeed, it is important to explore the extent to which the life course can be considered a social and cultural artifact. To what extent do social and cultural groupings construct and then prescribe the life-course patterns of their members? This is the theme of Chapter Five.

Chapter Five

The Life Course
as a Social Construct

Even the most casual observation reveals that age-graded norms, statuses, and roles are a feature of social organization. The concept of the life course (with its distinct phases or stages of infancy, childhood, adolescence, adulthood, and old age) is a central feature of modern Western society. We live in an age-graded society where much of social life is organized around socially standardized age categories. As a basic social institution, the life course has a material force; it may either impose external constraints on individual action (for example, sanctions for not behaving in an age-appropriate way), or, more importantly, shape the expectations we have about the proper progression of events and roles during our own life course, and ultimately the way in which we experience ourselves and our relations with others.

As a point of departure, it is worth noting some features and propositions about age structuring and how it relates to the life course of individuals. First, age structuring is influenced by history and culture. The life course is structured in different ways in different historical periods and in different cultures. While the fact of age structuring may be universal, it takes various forms in different cultures and historical periods. In this sense, the way age is structured is arbitrary rather than natural. Second, age structures, like other social structures such as gender and class, become embedded in the psychology of individuals. An understanding of the life course thus requires an understanding of how individuals engage—and struggle with—socially prescribed age categories. Third, socially constructed age categories change over time, as do the patterns of individual lives. But although individual and social change interrelate, they are not necessarily synchronized, which means there can be disjunctions between individual and social change—as when an individual becomes more concerned with moral and ethical issues in a society that is becoming increasingly materialist and competitive.

This chapter addresses these propositions in four sections. It commences with a section illustrating different historical and cultural conceptions of the life course. The idea of the social construction of the life course is then explored through an analogy with the social construction of gender. The third section focuses on the process through which age structuring is effected, and the final section looks at the implications for adult education theory and practice.

The Life Course in History and Culture

In different cultures and historical periods, there are different conceptions of the stages of life and their boundaries, dimensions, and divisions. There are different conceptions of the definition of a fully developed person, the processes through which development occurs, the significant tasks and marker events in life, the way certain stages of life are viewed, and the way development interacts with gender or class.

For example, Archard (1993) contrasts the Western and Oriental views of adulthood. In the Western view, adulthood is an achieved state, accomplished absolutely when childhood is left behind: "The adult is an individual who has grown up and achieved maturity. Adulthood is defined by the possession of properties which clearly and distinctly separate it from childhood" (p. 36). In contrast, the Oriental view holds that adulthood is a process whereby "the individual can become more and more of an adult, but there is no guarantee that ageing automatically brings with it maturity" (p. 36). In the previous chapter, we have seen that formal theories of adult development in Western culture certainly don't subscribe to the "adulthood as a state" point of view: that adulthood, once reached, is a stable state which continues for the remainder of one's life. But this theoretical interest in adulthood as a process is still relatively new, and perhaps it is true that the general social attitude in Western culture is that adulthood is a singular and stable end point of development—certainly this belief is reflected in law. Apart from this issue, some other comparisons between Oriental and Western views are worth pursuing. For example, Confucian thought has been documented in adult development texts, and it provides a good counterpoint to Western theory and social attitudes.

In the Confucian tradition, there is believed to be a magical connection between the ruler, the country as a whole, and its people. This is because all things share a common nature. Human development entails an unfolding of this nature, principally through diminishing the selfishness that separates us from others. Once we truly know our own nature, there is no difference between personal desire and what is morally correct. We learn to discover our own nature, and this is a lifelong endeavor. Even Confucius needed seventy years to develop to this stage:

> At fifteen I set my heart on learning;
>
> at thirty I took my stand;
>
> at forty I came to be free from doubts;
>
> at fifty I understood the Decree of Heaven;
>
> at sixty my ear was atuned;
>
> at seventy I followed my heart's desire without overstepping the line [cited in Lau, 1979, p. 121].

Ikels (1989) explains that after the twelfth century the ruler was no longer seen as the pivotal figure in the moral-cosmic drama. Thus the Neo-Confucianists turned from attempting to cultivate the ruler to cultivating themselves. Nevertheless, self-cultivation was still a matter of cultivating one's true, Heaven-bestowed nature, with its innate feelings and moral principles. Also, just as the ruler needed to receive instruction from the scholar-officials, so people must learn to cultivate the good in themselves. Because this "good" is a universal good, not subject to individual variation, it is not surprising to find that learning is said to occur through the repetition of performance and ritual behaviors. Ritual is what allows our innate feelings and correct motivations and actions to unfold as we manifest the Way.

The Confucian conception of self-cultivation is quite different from the Western popular ideal of cultivating the unique, distinctive qualities of the self. Wei-Ming (1978) also points to the absence of the adolescent phase in Confucian thought. Despite these differences, development along the Way does have elements in common with Western developmental theory, such as the paradoxical idea of being simultaneously related *and* detached from others. Wei-Ming explains: "So long as one's self image is mainly dependent upon the external responses of others, one's inner direction will be lost . . . steadfastness in the Confucian sense means the ability to remain unaffected by external influences in determining how one is to pursue and manifest the Way" (p. 118). Later, he adds, "Since a person in the Confucian sense is always a center of relationships rather than an *individual* complete in himself and separable from others, the structure and movement by which he expresses himself in the context of human relatedness becomes a defining characteristic of his humanity" (p. 120).

One need not look very far to find other parallels and contrasts between the way Western and non-Western cultures view the life course. For example, Sangree's study (1989) of the significance of parenthood and eldership among the Tiriki of Kenya and the Irigwe of Nigeria found that both these societies can be considered gerontocracies. Both accord very high status to their elders. However, he shows that parenthood is a prerequisite of high status for an older person in both these societies. This contrasts with the way we value and respect older people in Western society: we do so on the basis of what they have achieved in their lives—successful parenthood being neither necessary nor sufficient for respect. Sangree makes an interesting observation: "In the West the lives of the elderly are focused, as well as dependent, on their own pasts, to a degree that contrasts starkly with elders in Tiriki and Irigwe who feel strongly a part of their juniors' present and future. In Tiriki and Irigwe, the elderly's continuing involvement in and support of their children's and grandchildren's lives is a manifestation of those cultures' most cherished values and ideals" (p. 44).

Sangree goes on to observe that although progress and achievement are highly valued in Western societies, elderly people have relatively few—and minor—roles to play in the family and in society at large. They and their skills are seen as obsolescent. In contrast, Irigwe and Tiriki elders are not seen as obsolescent; rather, their social power grows throughout their life course, providing they contribute to the continuity of the family line.

Within Western culture, there are historical differences in the way the life course is viewed. Minois (1987), in his exhaustive *History of Old Age*, documents these historical differences, some of which mirror contemporary cultural differences. For example, in the early Middle Ages, Christian writers adopted the view that there is a solidarity between all the elements in the Universe—and that individual life is connected to the cosmos (a view shared with the Ionian philosophers of the sixth century B.C. and with the Confucians described above). St. Augustine, at the beginning of the fifth century A.D., developed the theme of the seven ages of the world (corresponding to the seven days of creation), and the seven ages of life.

It is also clear that in different historical periods there are different views about the stages of life. At the beginning of the seventh century, Isidore of Seville divided human life into six or seven parts, childhood (up to seven), pueritia (seven to fourteen), adolescence (fourteen to twenty-eight), youth (twenty-eight to fifty), maturity (fifty to seventy), and old age (beginning at seventy). Extending youth to the age of fifty is completely alien to the modern view, yet this division of the life span was adopted in the thirteenth century for inclusion in an encyclopedia purporting to contain the knowledge of the age—the *Magister de Proprietatibus Rerum,* "On the Properties of Things."

The aged are also seen quite differently in different historical periods. Minois (1987) once again summarizes the way social organization influences the social status of the old. There are five key elements:

1. *Extent of state protection.* When society falls into anarchy, and strong individuals and groups can do as they please, the elderly tend to suffer far more than in better-controlled states.

2. *Strength of the oral tradition.* In a society whose recollection of its history and procedures for dispute resolution rely on human memory, elderly people are valued more highly than they are in societies where the young believe they can find out everything they need for themselves.

3. *Valorization of physical beauty.* Where youthful physical beauty is the ideal, people place less value on the elderly than they do in societies whose view of beauty is more abstract and symbolic.

4. *Extended family.* Extended families tend to look after their own people throughout the life course, so elderly people fare better in societies where multigenerational households are the norm than in societies that favor the nuclear family.

5. *Creation of movable wealth.* Societies that place a high value on movable wealth allow some individuals to achieve great influence and maintain it well into old age but can also make it very difficult for elderly people without that wealth to survive.

There is always a certain amount of trade-off among these elements. For example, the anarchy of the early Middle Ages made life hard for elderly people, but the society's abstract and symbolic aesthetic ideal and its dependence on oral tradition served to some extent as a counterbalance. In addition, Minois adds that social class and wealth are general determinants of how well the aged are treated in society. Also, although it is not specifically mentioned, there is evidence that old women fare worse than old men. It is old women who are the target of particularly savage disparagement. Minois comments:

> The assimilation of the old woman into the ranks of malevolent powers was characteristic of the religious art of the fourteenth and fifteenth centuries. In representations of the Passion, an old woman appears as the incarnation of evil, leading the soldiers to the Mount of Olives and forging the nails for the Crucifixion. She can be seen in English miniatures shortly after 1300, in a French miniature of the "Pilgrimage of Jesus Christ" of 1393, in the "Hours of Etienne Chevalier" by Jean Fouquet, in a fifteenth-century mystery play, and in "The Mystery of the Passion" by Jean Michel, in which she is called Hedroit, is ugly and loathes Jesus [p. 231].

Overall, Minois argues, there has never been a golden age for the old, because the favorable factors have never combined in any one historical period: gains in one area have generally been offset by deterioration in another.

The other end of the age spectrum, childhood, has also been the subject of historical analysis. The seminal work was *Centuries of Childhood,* by Philippe Ariès (1962). Ariès argues that "In medieval society the idea of childhood did not exist; this is not to suggest that children were neglected, forsaken or despised. The idea of childhood is not to be confused with affection for children: it corresponds to an awareness of the particular nature of childhood, that particular nature which distinguishes the child from the adult, even the young adult. In medieval society this awareness was lacking" (p. 125).

Ariès observed that children were represented in paintings as miniature adults, there were no separate children's games as there are now, and they were not protected from sexually immodest language. The deaths of infant children were also treated in a more casual way than in present times. In the present, children are recognized as separate from the adult world in many ways: they have different games, different clothes, they learn and play in separate spaces, they are innocent and the adult world is knowing. In responding to Ariès's thesis, Archard (1993) argues that it was not so much that previous society lacked a concept of childhood; it simply lacked *our* concept of childhood. Nevertheless, he agrees that childhood as a stage of the life cycle is conceived differently in different historical periods.

We make the above cultural and historical observations in order to introduce and illustrate the proposition that the life course is, at least partly, an invention of social groupings: it is in this sense that it can be considered to be a social construct like other social categories such as gender and class. The following section takes this idea a little further.

Parallels Between the Social Construction of Age and Gender

Arguably, we locate ourselves as belonging to an age category in much the same way that we locate ourselves as being masculine or feminine. It is worthwhile then to explore some of the parallels, differences, and intersections between gender identity and age identity.

State intervention and regulation have historically served to maintain distinctions of both gender and age category. With respect to the life course, the state legalizes, standardizes and provides institutional support for entry into and exit from formal education, employment, marriage, and even life itself (through birth and death certificates). There are a range of supporting mechanisms that distribute resources and opportunities to ensure an orderly progression through the various age categories and divisions within them. For example, there are regulations concerning the commencement, progression, and termination of schooling; funds are provided to assist with the immediate transition from secondary schooling to post-secondary education; scholarships, apprenticeships, and job search schemes are often targeted toward a particular age category; mandatory retirement is combined with superannuation and other retirement schemes; and there are a host of welfare services targeted toward particular age groups. Non-state-controlled institutions also spread opportunities and resources to enhance an individual's progression through a socially approved, age-based timetable of "successful" career, family, or personal development. This institutionalization of age, and the co-optation of society at large, makes it highly unlikely that individuals can chart alternative life courses—at least without considerable financial or personal cost.

There are forces moving against the continued institutionalization of the life course. Factors such as demographic and technological change, changes in male/female relations, and changes in the way work is organized do raise questions as to the extent to which society will continue to be age-graded in postmodern times. However, the essential point is that the state clearly has an interest in demarcating the roles, responsibilities, and demands made on different age categories.

Second, in order to function effectively as members of late twentieth-century Western society, we need to identify correctly the gender and age categories to which others belong, and to assist others in identifying us as well. This is because our interactions with others are partly based upon presumptions about gender or age. In the instance of gender, there are (among children at least) very few observable physical differences in most public situations. Parents teach children to position themselves by gender using signifiers such as dress, hairstyle, topics of conversation, and choices of activity. The physical differences associated with age categories are perhaps more obvious, but nevertheless the same types of signifiers apply. Thus we speak of dress, hairstyle, and activity as age-inappropriate in much the same way that we speak of them in relation to gender.

Furthermore, as with gender, one develops a posture and attitude toward oneself as belonging to an age category. By this, we mean the adoption of psychological characteristics deemed to be appropriate for a given age, to satisfy general social expectations that at least partially govern relations among age categories. Failure to act in an age-appropriate manner is seen as deviant by others, who at best will react with mild amusement, perplexity, or perhaps a few patronizing comments, and at worst with anger, fear, or moral outrage. These expectations can be very powerful, leading some young adults to behave as though they feel bold and some elderly ones to behave timidly, despite personal inclinations to the contrary.

Third, just as gender is seen as a product of biological sex differences, age categories are seen as the natural result of physiological and biological factors associated with chronological age. There are two issues here, the first concerning the nature of physiological and biological change throughout the life course, and the second concerning the relation between these changes and age-appropriate behavior. Much of our conception of age-appropriate behavior is based upon presumed physiological correlates of age categories, especially during the years from early adulthood until old age. The general popular image is one of developing cognitive and social competence throughout childhood, then one of decline in physiological function throughout adulthood: a decline in vision, hearing, taste, and smell; a slowing of the central nervous system; loss of skin elasticity, muscle, and subcutaneous fat; increasing skeletal brittleness and a corresponding loss of stature. These changes are said to lead to a susceptibility to disease and accidents, a decline in performance on perceptual, motor and intellectual tasks, and increasing dependency, psychological withdrawal, and social isolation.

However, except among the very elderly, or among those with chronic disease or impairment, these physiological changes do not significantly affect most areas of human activity, at least within the normal range of function. There is now greater recognition of individual differences, generational effects, compensatory mechanisms, and the positive impact of social intervention. For example, many of the changes attributed to aging are more properly considered the result of disease. Also, summary statistics showing that aged populations have a higher incidence of chronic disease and impairment may be partly explained by generational differences in health care opportunities. And finally, some of the indicators of dependence may be susceptible to social intervention. For example, incontinence in the elderly, which is often used as a basis for consignment to nursing homes, can be partly prevented by training, by refusing to label the person as incontinent, and by improving access to the toilet (Williams, 1983, cited in Riley, 1987). At the other end of the age spectrum, a similar mythology prevails. The image is one of slowly emerging competence throughout the years of early childhood until about middle childhood (eight years of age). Before then, children are thought to be incapable of even the most simple logical, deductive thinking. They are said to be egocentric, unable to deduce what other people think and feel. The egocentric young child is also said to believe that objects cease to exist when out of sight. However, there is a growing awareness that this concept of young children underestimates their intelligence and abilities. The point is that simple developmental formulas contribute to myths about age-appropriate behavior and undervalue the capacities of those at the extremes of the developmental spectrum.

In summary, the physiological and biological factors associated with aging are not sufficient to support existing conceptions of age-appropriate behavior. There also is little evidence, except for the very old and the very young, for a direct connection between chronological age and the constraints imposed by our conception of age-appropriate behavior.

The fourth point of comparison we wish to make with gender identity has to do with understanding the processes and structures underlying the emergence and maintenance of age-category identity. The concern here is not with why age categories seem to be a feature of social organization, but rather with how we come to constitute ourselves as belonging to a particular age category.

To begin with, it seems reasonable to consider age category, like gender, to be primarily a social phenomenon. It has no direct physiological or biological basis, and as a social phenomenon, it is historically and culturally specific. How then is age category transmitted to new generations, and what processes change the way it is constituted? The position adopted here is that social phenomena are not transmitted genetically; they are transmitted socially and symbolically.

In the life course of any individual, social phenomena like gender and age category are historical givens. They are arbitrary in the sense that they are human creations, but they are nevertheless experienced as objectively real in much the same way that physical objects are experienced as real or natural. But whereas the physical world is experienced through perceiving and acting on things, the social world is experienced through interactions with others and through exposure to social institutions. In a sense, we come to *know* the physical world, but we come to *be* the social world.

It is by interacting with others, and reacting to or participating in social institutions—most importantly through symbolic processes—that we come to constitute ourselves as social beings. Accepting this position, our argument is that there is a discourse pertinent to age category in much the same way that there is a discourse pertinent to gender. Like gender, age category is sustained as a seemingly natural element of personal identity and subjective experience by learning the discursive practices in which members of one's culture are positioned on an age-graded continuum (Davies, 1989). Furthermore, gender and age category intersect. The male life course is constructed very differently from the female life course, and gender-based relations of dominance and power are embedded in the discourse associated with age categories (Gilligan, 1986).

If discourse lies at the heart of the process, how is change possible? It seems that it is only possible through adopting new and different forms of discourse. But this is not an easy solution, given the strength of psychological constraints (repression) and the coercive nature of the social structure (oppression).

Before proceeding, some of the differences between age category and gender warrant attention—they may have implications for understanding the processes involved. The first and most obvious difference between gender and age category is that gender is bipolar, whereas age category is a continuum. A person must move from one age category to another with the passage of time, a transformation which is patently not a feature of gender. Some commentators argue that gender is sustained through a discourse that portrays the individual self as being unitary, coherent, and unchanging in certain ways, especially in being male or female (Davies, 1989). At first glance, this conception does not seem to apply to the life course: quite the contrary, the discourse associated with age category appears to be one where the individual is portrayed as being in process, with a subjectivity that is at times precarious and contradictory (as in Levinson's basic tensions, 1978). However, underlying the concept of age category is a discourse that views the individual as developing in a way that preserves stability, equilibrium, and balance in the self. This discourse thus seems similar to the one supporting gender difference. At the core of developmental process is the individual subject, whose continuity and coherence has a temporal aspect which limits past, present, and future. One's age category is not set in the same way that gender is set. However, the unfolding of one's development is set, and departures from this are interpreted as failure to grow.

The prospect of moving from one age to another means that one's positioning in a given age category is tentative, or at least temporally bound (unlike the case with gender). Because age category is a continuum, the boundaries of appropriate behavior have a measure of uncertainty or ambiguity. Through fantasy, play, or future plans, we position ourselves to adopt the characteristics of future age categories, we are encouraged as children to prepare for schooling or to "make believe" an adult world, as adolescents to prepare for a career, as working adults to prepare for retirement, and as retirees to prepare for senescence, disability, and decline. Our early preparation for anticipated roles in later life may eventually be disrupted by social changes that alter these roles as we come to fill them. For example, many women raised in the fifties in anticipation of being housewives in the seventies were instead faced with new social expectations for participation in the paid workforce—a clear conflict between psychological anticipation and preparation on the one hand, and contemporary conditions on the other.

In daily interaction with people, we position ourselves in relation to each other, and it is partly through understanding the position of others that our own position is defined. However, in the case of age category, we also position ourselves with a view to *becoming* the other. In this way we learn to position ourselves on a life-span trajectory. Much of the literature on life-span psychological development seeks to describe and explain the dynamics of this trajectory (*normative life events*) or disruptions to this trajectory at the individual level (*nonnormative life events*). However, disruptions to this trajectory are social and historical, as well as idiosyncratic to individuals. Economic, technological, and social change have an impact on life-course trajectories en masse, and often demand substantial psychological readjustment and the adoption of new discursive practices among those affected—with many casualties.

The argument is that chronological age has no necessary implication for the subjective positioning of any individual. Furthermore, age categories, structured in the current manner, limit and unnecessarily constrain what should be an open nexus of possibilities across the life span (Davies, 1989, p. 12).

Implications of "Adulthood as a Social Construct"

Adult educators who seek to make their work of individual change and transformation fit into a wider agenda of social change and transformation need to acknowledge the social and historical dimension of adult development. This perception will help them distinguish learning experiences and personal changes that genuinely transform and liberate their students from those that simply key into the social expectations associated with different phases of life. The importance of this distinction can be illustrated by a review of Mezirow's theory of perspective transformation and in the links he makes between perspective transformation and adult development. We choose Mezirow because of the influence of his ideas, and because he grapples with the problem of personal and social transformation. We seek to advance his ideas through a critique of the way he links perspective transformation and life-span development.

Specifically, we argue that Mezirow does not sufficiently explore the social origins of the life course, which leads him to find instances of perspective transformation in growth events that we would call normative psychological development. In discussing these observations, he refers mainly to psychological theories of development, such as those of Bruner, Piaget, Gould, Levinson, Erikson, Perry, Labouvie-Vief, and others, all of whom are concerned with identifying the phases, stages, and processes of adult development. Now, *development* implies growth and progress, not merely change. But growth and progress toward what end? It is the conception of the end point of development, the mature or healthy personality, that determines how developmental progress is defined. This conception cannot be divorced from issues of social value. Drawing from an extensive literature, Mezirow's position (1991a) is clear: "The test of a developmentally progressive perspective is not only that it is more inclusive, discriminating, and integrative of experience but also that it is permeable (open) to alternative perspectives so that inclusivity, discrimination, and integration continually increase" (p. 156).

This formulation, however, needs to acknowledge that what is (and what is not) more "integrative of experience" depends on the social and historical context in which the experience occurs. As indicated earlier, Gilligan (1986) drew attention to the way developmental theories undervalue the qualities that serve to integrate the experiences of women, such as an increased capacity for empathy and attachment. Instead, she argues, existing theories concentrate on qualities such as autonomy, individuation, and independence, which serve to integrate the experiences of men. The point is that what constitutes psychological development is legitimately contested, and makes little sense without reference to social and historical circumstances and processes. Many normative life cycle changes may be *experienced* as being fundamental changes in world view—when in reality they fit quite neatly into expected life cycle patterns like the changes associated with leaving the parental home, marrying, or having a child. Such changes are more accurately portrayed as changes in an individual's *location* within an overarching taken-for-granted world view. This is not to underestimate the significance of these events for the individual, it is only to make the point that normative life cycle changes do not *require* the questioning of the premises underlying what is expected. Mezirow (1991a) does not explicitly address this distinction between normative and fundamentally transformative change in relation to adult development, but he does make an important and relevant theoretical distinction between the transformation of "meaning schemes"—the procedures by which a person absorbs new information or techniques—and transformation of "meaning *perspectives*". He writes:

> The transformation of meaning schemes is integral to the process of reflection. As we assess our assumptions about the content or process of problem solving and find them unjustified, we create new ones or transform our old assumptions and hence our interpretations of experience. This is the dynamics of everyday reflective learning. When occasionally we are forced to assess or reassess the basic premises we have taken for granted and find them unjustified, perspective transformation, followed by major life changes, may result [p. 192].

The transformation of meaning schemes is somehow less fundamental than perspective transformation proper. The former implies development and progress within a taken-for-granted world view. The latter implies development resulting from the exposure and deconstruction of a given world view and its replacement by a new world view. This distinction is important, but it needs further elaboration in Mezirow's theory. It is important because it signals two very different types of development and learning: reflective learning, which leads to a transformation of meaning schemes, and transformative learning, which leads to a transformation of meaning perspectives.

For example, consider Arin-Krupp's observation (1990) that in the first half of life, men are generally more assertive than women and women are more nurturing than men, while in the second half of life men become more nurturing and women become more assertive—a point well documented in the literature: see Hyde and Phillips, 1979; and Gutmann, 1987. Adult educators could respond to this developmental trend toward reversing assertiveness roles by introducing appropriate courses, methodologies, and materials to enhance and support it. Learners might be encouraged to reflect on their beliefs, attitudes, and emotional reactions, or they might even practice the skills associated with "assertiveness" and "nurturing" as appropriate. However, if confined in this way, the role of the adult educator would simply be adaptive: a support to a socially produced phase or stage of the life course. In Mezirow's terms, this life-cycle change would correspond to a transformation of meaning schemes. However, adult educators could go further and encourage critical reflection on the social and historical origins of this gender difference and the internalized premises on which the difference is based. The life-cycle change would then be located within the larger context of how gender identity is formed and whose interests it serves. This has the potential to dramatically alter the perception and interpretation of the experience from one that simply marks a phase of the life cycle to one that endows meaning to, and validates, one's life history. Such a change, which truly integrates experience, would correspond to Mezirow's concept of perspective transformation.

The distinction between the transformation of meaning schemes and meaning perspectives is most clearly apparent in the contrasting approaches of Gould and Hart, both of whom are contributors to Mezirow's edited volume *Fostering Critical Reflection in Adulthood* (1990). Gould (1990) has this to say in introducing his contribution, the chapter entitled "The Therapeutic Learning Program:"

When adults develop, they have to learn how to adapt to a whole new set of circumstances as they go through life's transitions. . . .

An adaptational response is required to meet some demand implicit in a situational context, and that context is frequently cat-alogued as either a transition, a crisis, a stress situation, or a challenge. All people change with age because new priorities in the life cycle require new attitudes and new behavior. . . .

Sometimes people cannot respond to the fact of current reality with the appropriate adaptation because that response is mired in internal conflict [pp. 134–136].

Gould portrays development as an adaptation to the changed expectations and circumstances associated with different life phases. For him, psychological health and development are expressed in terms of how well the individual adapts to society's needs—there is no social critique or analysis. Thus it is not society that is problem-atic; any problems belong to the individuals who cannot adapt properly to society's requirements. The possibility that there are some forms of social organization that are alienating or oppressive is not addressed. Thus, although Gould is describing a legitimately developmental phenomenon, his view of development seems to run directly *counter* to the spirit of perspective transformation (although the phenomenon he describes may qualify as a transformation of meaning schemes).

Hart's analysis (1990) in "Liberation Through Consciousness Raising" stands in stark contrast to the above example. She com-mences her description of consciousness raising in women's groups with a treatment of the historical context in which consciousness raising groups first formed. She understands, and is at pains to point out, the trap of psychologizing a phenomenon which is both social and psychological: "The real danger lay in getting stuck in the per-sonal by focusing on the individual woman herself instead of mov-ing on and outward to a collective analysis of the situation of women. The danger therefore did not reside in the topic itself, but in the group members' inability or unwillingness to see an experience or problem as testimony for a general state of affairs rather than as an individual problem calling for individual solutions" (p. 54).

Hart's description and analysis of the main principles and characteristics of consciousness raising is in keeping with the implied more radical (in the sense of "going to the root or origin") intent of perspective transformation: "The power of consciousness raising derives in large measure from its spontaneity and from its roots in a sociopolitical movement of liberation. It ignites around the theme of oppression, presupposes a certain view about knowledge and knowing that empowers rather than extinguishes the individual knower, and calls for a relationship between theory and practice that begins with a however vaguely felt or articulated acknowledgment of power and finishes with a systematic understanding of the nature and complexity of the entire power-bound social reality" (p. 70).

Thus Hart also describes a developmental phenomenon, consciousness raising, but does so in a way that exemplifies the radical intent of perspective transformation by linking individual experience and individual psychology to collective experiences, and ultimately to a critical understanding of the relation between the individual and society.

Adult education for transformation of the type described above can be considered a version of what Foucault (1988) refers to as a "technology of the self"—an observation also made by Usher, 1993. According to Foucault, technologies of the self form one of four groups of technologies; the others being technologies of production, sign systems, and power. Technologies of the self "permit individuals to effect by their own means or with the help of others a certain number of operations on their bodies and souls, thoughts, conduct, and way of being, so as to transform themselves in order to attain a certain state of happiness, purity, wisdom, perfection, or immortality" (p. 18).

Foucault further observes that there are three major types of self-examination: how our thoughts relate to reality, how our thoughts relate to rules, and finally, how our thoughts relate to—and reveal—our inner selves. The last of these implies something hidden and leading to self-illusion. Early Christian thought emphasized disclosing the self, that is, showing the truth about oneself, through penance, or through the continual verbalization of thoughts in obedience to a master. In either case, disclosure of the self is tantamount to renunciation of the self. "The theme of self renunciation is very important. Throughout Christianity there is a correlation between disclosure of the self, dramatic or verbalized, and the renunciation of the self. My hypothesis from looking at these two techniques is that it's the second one, verbalization, which becomes the more important." He adds, "From the eighteenth century to the present, the techniques of verbalization have been reinserted in a different context by the so-called human sciences in order to use them without renunciation of the self but to constitute, positively, a new self" (1988, pp. 48–49).

Clearly, adult education for transformation fits within this secular version of self-disclosure in that its purpose is to reconstruct the self rather than to renounce the self. Foucault, like many adult educators, stresses the need to criticize ourselves and the world. However, the nature of our criticism must be thoroughly historicist; our critique, in his view, while acknowledging the contingent nature of our being, must at the same time admit the possibility of becoming other than what we are. It is this kind of transformation that gives impetus to the work of freedom.

Thus the task is not discovering who one truly is, but inventing, improvising, and creating who one can be.

Conclusion

The argument advanced in this chapter is that the life course, as a product of history and culture, is socially constructed, and that therefore individual development should be considered both a social and a personal phenomenon. From the point of view of the adult educator concerned with personal transformation, it is thus necessary to distinguish learning experiences that are fundamentally transformative and emancipatory (involving some level of social critique) from those that are simply part of the social expectations associated with different phases of the life cycle. While perspective transformation, in Mezirow's sense, implies development, the converse is not necessarily true. This is because much of what is regarded as "normal" development occurs within a framework of taken-for-granted assumptions about the world.

Perspective transformation, however, is a process which challenges these assumptions. As such, it represents a developmental *shift* (a new world view) rather than simply developmental *progress*. Adult education researchers and practitioners need to recognize this distinction in order to avoid the inappropriate application of perspective transformation to instances of normal development. Also, adult educators who work in areas where there is a link between personal and social change (for example, migrant education, literacy programs, labor education, the education of indigenous people, racism and sexism workshops, programs for the unemployed) and who wish to realize the radical intent of perspective transformation, need to be mindful of the ways in which the life course is socially constructed both in theory and in the lives of individuals. The danger of omitting a social and historical critique when theorizing about or engaging in education for perspective transformation, is that, in the absence of such a critique, conventionally held views of what it means to be "enlightened" or "developmentally more mature" may dominate and subvert the process.

Chapter Six

Promoting Autonomy and Self-Direction

The idea of autonomous or self-directed learning is firmly entrenched in contemporary thinking about adult education, and there has been a great deal of scholarly interest in the subject. There are now a variety of meanings attached to the term autonomy, particularly the dimensions along which autonomy is exercised. For example, Gibbs (1979) distinguishes between the intellectual and moral dimensions of autonomy. The former is equated with "critical intelligence, independence of thought and judgement, discernment, [and] . . . a readiness to think things out for oneself free from bias and prejudice. . . ." (p. 121). Moral autonomy refers to a "disposition of character rather than intellect: self-mastery or self-discipline, having command of one's own feelings and inclinations . . . where . . . self-mastery is conceived as something like what used to be called fortitude" (pp. 121–122). Crittenden (1978) regards autonomy as having three important dimensions: intellectual, moral, and emotional. He writes:

> Under the intellectual I include the whole range of one's beliefs, whether they are about the nature of the world or the things that are thought to be worthwhile or the standards of conduct. At an extreme limit intellectual autonomy would require in the first place that a person not accept any of his important beliefs primarily on the authority of others, but on his own experience, his own reflection on evidence and argument, his own sense of what is true and right. For complete intellectual autonomy it would also seem necessary that a person should determine . . . what constitutes a true

claim, adequate evidence, a justifiable moral principle, and the like. . . . Moral autonomy, as I am using the expression, is intended to embrace all forms of practical judgement and action. . . . In addition to independence of thought in determining and applying criteria of moral judgment, moral autonomy also includes the executive capacities for carrying into practice what one decides should be done. The possession of these capacities is commonly described by such terms as tenacity, resoluteness, strength of will, self-mastery. The third main aspect of autonomy, the emotional may be treated as part of self-mastery. . . . However, the point is not simply that a person would exercise self-mastery in the face of strong emotional involvement, but that he or she would remain emotionally detached in relationships with other persons and things. This form of independence and self-sufficiency has a long history as an ideal. It was illustrated in the life of Socrates and cultivated as a central doctrine by the Cynics and the Stoics [pp. 107–108].

Partridge (1979) asserts that the autonomous person has three qualities: freedom of choice (an absence of internal or external coercion), rational reflection (the ability to arrive at reasons for behavior based on objective evidence), and strength of will (not diverted by whims and impulses).

Finally, Philip Candy, in his comprehensive analysis "Self-Direction for Lifelong Learning" (1991), explores the relationship between autonomy as a learner (that is, one's capacity to pursue learning in a self-directed manner) and autonomy as a general personal attribute. The term self-direction in learning, he argues, embraces four distinct phenomena: personal autonomy, the willingness and capacity to manage one's own learning, an environment allowing some effective control by the learner, and the independent pursuit of learning without formal institutional support or affiliation. He recognizes that self-direction is conceived both as a process whereby learners obtain control or assistance for their learning, and as an ideal end point where "self-directedness" in some wider sense is developed: "The development of self-directed individuals—that is, people who exhibit the qualities of moral, emotional, and intellectual autonomy—is the long term goal of most, if not all, educational endeavors. As such, it has a long and distinguished history in the philosophy of education" (1991, p. 19). While the tension is normally portrayed as being between autonomy and dependence, particularly dependence on the teacher, there is another way of thinking about the tension. Rather than a matter of individual relationships, dependence can be seen as a general state of affairs characterizing a group or section of society, and interfering with the development of freedom and self-determination for that group.

It is important to keep the above facets of autonomy and self-direction in mind when exploring some of the issues addressed in the literature, such as the nature and development of the capacities which underpin autonomy and self-direction, the question of whether autonomous and self-directed learning is a general or domain-specific attribute, and the limits and desirability of autonomy as a general personal attribute or quality of the self. These issues form the framework for the rest of this chapter.

Development of the Capacity for Autonomy and Self-Direction

Is there a link between self-directed learning techniques and strategies and the development of personal autonomy? What other kinds of experiences lead to the development of personal autonomy? Conversely, is there a link between the development of personal autonomy and the capacity to be a self-directed learner?

The views of autonomy mentioned at the outset have in common the emphasis on the capacity to think rationally, reflect, analyze evidence, and make judgments; to know oneself and be free to form and express one's own opinions; and finally, to be able to act in the world. We have seen in earlier chapters how these qualities appear in various guises in the psychological literature on adult development, and how more recent conceptualizations of intelligence, along with challenges to the social and cultural bias of developmental theories, serve to modify or extend the concept of autonomy. There also exists a literature describing development in terms of attitudes and views of education and knowledge. This literature makes an explicit link between development and the capacity for autonomous learning. It includes the pioneering work of Perry (1968) on intellectual and ethical development during college years, wherein he documents stages in the development of students' conceptions of what constitutes knowledge. It also includes the work of Weathersby (1981), who relates Loevinger's stages of ego development to stages in the conception of the meaning and purpose of education. He used a sentence-completion test to elicit the links between students' ego stage and conception of education. At the lowest stage, students see education as some kind of product, external to the self and acquired by school attendance. By contrast, at the highest stage they see education as an open-ended and intrinsically valuable process within the self, leading to a better understanding of self and others.

Here are Weathersby's education ego stages:

Impulsive and Self-Protective Stages

Education is viewed as a *thing* that you get in school and then have. Positive remarks are undifferentiated. There are also expressions of distaste for education, or of not getting along in school.

Conformist Stage

Education is generally interpreted as school attendance, which has practical usefulness; one can get a better job with it than without it. An uncritical, idealized view of education is expressed, in which the current number of years of schooling is considered necessary for everyone.

Self-Aware Stage

Education's importance is viewed in terms of one's life or future. There is a shift away from thinking of education as a concrete entity toward thinking of it as a goal and an asset.

Conscientious Stage

Education is viewed as an experience that affects a person's inner life. It is no longer merely a prescribed number of years useful schooling. Its importance lies in intellectual stimulation and enrichment. It influences a person's whole life, making it more worthwhile and enjoyable. Education is an opportunity that should be available to everyone. It is seen as being a significant force in improving society, though the educational system may be seen as needing improvement as well.

Individualistic Stage

This view has an element of both the conscientious and autonomous perspectives; conscientious themes are more fully elaborated, and the focus is shifting to education as a lifelong process essential for a full life.

Autonomous and Integrated Stages

Education is seen as leading to a deeper understanding of oneself and others, as helping to cope with life, as leading to creativity, self-fulfilment, and deeper values; hence, education is intrinsically valuable. It is not a thing one has or gets, once and for all, nor is it identified solely with school and intellectual achievement apart from interpersonal relations and emotional involvements [Weathersby, 1981, pp. 61–62, adapted].

Weathersby argues that learners at different stages of ego development have different assumptions (and therefore expectations) about the purpose and potential of education, different capacities to frame educational goals, and different interpretations of the meaning of educational experiences. Thus teachers need to understand how the ego stage influences the learners' responses to educational intervention. This understanding can be used partly to understand the learners' perspectives, partly to accommodate those perspectives, and partly to challenge and promote the further development of those perspectives toward the autonomous and integrated stage.

"Exposure to higher level reasoning, opportunities to take others' roles and perspectives, discomforting discrepancies between one's actual experiences in a situation and one's current explanations and beliefs—these are the basic elements of the transition process. . . . The basic principle is to create a course structure in which the assignments and interpersonal interactions foster ego development . . ." (1981, pp. 71-72).

For Weathersby, education is inextricably bound up with developmental change, and teaching practices need to take into account the developmental capacity and potential of learners. A developmental framework also provides the teacher with a better grasp of how learners interpret and make use of educational experiences.

More recently, the work of Usher (1985, 1989) and Kitchener and King (1991, 1994) follows this tradition and applies it more specifically to adult education.

Usher, in a series of related papers on experience and learning, explores (among other things) the nature and acquisition of those prior skills, attitudes, and attributes that make learning from experience possible. The development of reflective skills, that is, the ability to select from and problematize experience, is considered the key. But what lies behind these skills and how are they acquired? Usher sees a link between the way students use their experience and the conceptions they hold about the nature of learning and knowledge. Drawing upon an earlier study by Säljö (1979), he makes a distinction between two different conceptions of learning and knowledge, as shown in Table 6.1.

Usher argues that a reproductive conception of learning and a dualistic conception of knowledge lead to a "surface" approach where experience is deemed anecdotal, trivial, or irrelevant to learning. In contrast, a thematized conception of learning and a perspective-dependent conception of knowledge lead to a "deep" or productive use of experience. He further argues that whether one develops a deep or surface approach to learning from experience is greatly influenced by the learning and teaching "to which one is exposed," and concludes, "In any course of study the

Table 6.1. Approaches to Experience in Learning.

Approaches to experience	Conceptions of learning	Conceptions of knowledge
Surface	Reproductive—learning is considered a matter of acquiring and reproducing a body of knowledge.	Dualistic—knowledge is considered "right" or "wrong" as determined by experts.
Deep	Thematized—learning is viewed as contextual and the learner is aware of the learning process.	Perspective dependent— knowledge is seen as dependent upon a stand-point and context.

Source: Adapted from Usher, 1985.

nature of learning tasks can be such as to encourage and reinforce reproductive/dualistic conceptions of learning and knowledge. This occurs most obviously where the academic nature of learning tasks is stressed . . . learning tasks which are experienced-focused rather than academic will reinforce thematised, perspective-dependent conceptions and encourage deep level (productive) as against surface level (anecdotal) approaches to using experience" (1985, pp. 67–68).

He adds a cautionary note here, saying that it is difficult to establish a genuine student-centered, participative, and experiential teaching strategy in an environment where the emphasis is on the expertise and authority of the teacher. Nevertheless, the thrust of Usher's argument is that exposure to genuine experiential learning influences a student's conception of learning and knowledge in a way that allows experience to be used productively in future learning.

Kitchener and King (1991, 1994) offer an analysis similar to Usher's, but they describe seven stages in their reflective judgment model, as follows. Their research is based on the Reflective Judgment Interview (Kitchener and King, 1991). The interview requires subjects to analyze four ill-structured problems that sample the dilemmas of knowing in historical, scientific, religious, and everyday contexts. For example, the interviewee may be presented with a number of explanations of, say, the building of the pyramids in ancient Egypt. The interviewer then asks a series of probe questions such as, "What do you think about these statements?" "How did you come to hold that point of view?" "On what do you base that point of view?" And finally, "How is it that experts in the field disagree about this subject?"

Kitchener and King's Stages of Reflective Judgment

Stage 1. Knowledge is absolute and concrete, based on direct observation. There is no recognition of problems for which there are no absolutely true answers. In its pure form this stage is found only in young children.

Stage 2. Not everyone knows the truth, although it is ultimately accessible to all, and therefore all problems are solvable. The problem is simply to find the right source for an answer—a teacher or parent, for example. This frame of reference is typical of young adolescents.

Stage 3. There is a recognition that truth, even for those in authority, may be temporarily inaccessible. Either there is concrete evidence or there is not, in which case all we have is what feels right at the moment. Without concrete evidence, there is no acknowledgment of the possibility of evaluating beliefs beyond the feelings one may have. Students in the last two years of high school and in the first year of college typically score at this stage.

Stage 4. The uncertainty of knowing is acknowledged, but there is a corresponding sense of confusion about how to make knowledgeable claims in the light of this uncertainty. The result may be a certain skepticism about the role of authorities. There is a growing distinction between well-structured problems, which can be solved with certainty, and ill-structured problems, where there is not a single solution.

Stage 5. There is a belief that knowledge must be placed in a context, mainly because interpretation plays a role in what a person perceives. Interpretation is required to justify an explanation, although it is not really possible to evaluate the worth of differing interpretations. This type of reasoning is most typical of graduate students.

Stage 6. In addition to recognizing the importance of context, those at this level regard knowing as involving an evaluation of the relative worth of differing perspectives or points of view. These evaluations involve comparing evidence and opinions across contexts, which is typically found among advanced graduate students.

Stage 7. There is a belief that one can make justifiable claims about the better or best solution to a problem through critical inquiry and by synthesizing existing evidence and opinion. Individuals argue that such views can be offered as reasonable current solutions to the problems at hand.

There is evidence that the stages described by Kitchener and King are sequential, that they correlate highly with age, and that they are linked to educational attainment, but also that they are relatively independent of intelligence or cognitive stage.

Kitchener and King see five implications for educators in these findings. First, educators can assume that students will approach ill-structured problems according to their stage of reflective judgment—therefore their stages should be monitored and teaching practices adjusted accordingly. Second, because there are age-related developmental ceilings, educators should be wary of assuming that younger students are capable of reflective judgment: "Even among a college-educated sample, the majority did not typically use reasoning higher than stage four prior to age twenty-four" (1991, p. 167). Third, because the stages are sequential, educators should not employ exercises or techniques which require skills beyond one level higher than a particular student's reflective judgment stage.

Fourth, educators should use ill-structured problems to help promote reflective judgment. Finally, learning that leads to developmental progress causes disequilibrium as old frames of reference are challenged—therefore educators need to both challenge old perspectives and support the acquisition of new perspectives. They describe the type of teaching intervention they have in mind when aiming to promote development from one stage to the next:

> It is difficult for those using Stage Five reasoning to evaluate competing evidence-based interpretations that reflect different points of view on an issue. It is hard for them to identify relationships between points of view and to act as though each were discrete. These individuals also have difficulty endorsing one view as better than another, as if doing so would deny the legitimacy of other perspectives. Consequently, the most important learning objective for those at this stage is to relate alternative points of view to each other, comparing the evidence and opinion for each in order to arrive at a conclusion that integrates the alternatives or evaluates one as better or best in a limited sense. Further, individuals must acknowledge that such conclusions need not sacrifice the appreciation for multiple perspectives that is the hallmark of Stage Five reasoning. [Possible assignments that make this goal explicit are listed below.]
>
> 1. Compare and contrast two competing points of view, citing and evaluating evidence and arguments used by proponents of each. Determine which author makes the better interpretation of the evidence and which conclusion is most appropriate.
>
> 2. Select a controversial issue from those discussed in class. Explain at least two points of view from which the issue has been addressed by scholars. Indicate which point of view you believe to be the most appropriate and the grounds for that decision [1991, pp. 170–171].

Although Kitchener and King, and Usher, identify developmental levels which are entirely compatible, the implications they draw for teaching are quite different. While Usher stresses the need to institute student-centered and experiential learning, Kitchener and King seem to assume a rather traditional academic setting whereby the teacher models the desirable thought processes and sets assignments to test and challenge the thought processes of students. In some ways it is ironic that Kitchener and King use ill-structured problems in their research, the types of problems that one encounters in everyday settings, and then advocate assignments to develop the capacity to reason about these ill-structured problems. They seem to be caught in a bind: on one hand, their notion of reflective judgment captures quite nicely the kind of practical intelligence discussed in earlier chapters; but on the other hand, the evidence points to formal education as promoting the acquisition of reflective judgment. Indeed, they report that adult students entering college for the first time tend to be at the same stage as younger students at a similar educational level—this implies that experience of real-world problems does not enhance one's capacity for reflective judgment. Such a view is not only counter-intuitive, it stands in stark contrast to the findings on the acquisition of practical intelligence, expertise, and tacit knowledge discussed earlier. This contradiction can perhaps be resolved by recognizing that whereas practical intelligence is largely domain specific, reflective judgment is considered a generic capacity— while the problems being thought about are ill-structured they remain context free and therefore the language used to analyze them is more abstract and academic.

Autonomous and Self-Directed Learning: General or Domain-Specific?

To what extent is the capacity for autonomous learning a general attribute, operating independently of the subject matter or the context in which learning occurs? There have been many attempts to identify the general characteristics of the autonomous or self-directed learner and the role of the teacher in promoting such a learner. Some commentators, such as Knowles (1978), argue that teachers of adults should use techniques that build upon adults' natural capacity and desire to plan and conduct their own learning. This means that the role of the teacher becomes that of a facilitator of learning, that is, one who assists learners to formulate goals and objectives, locate appropriate resources, plan learning strategies, and evaluate the outcomes of learning. Thus, self-directed learning is characterized by the mastery of a set of techniques and procedures for learning, and the role of the teacher is to assist students to "learn how to learn." Candy (1991), after an extensive literature review, identifies a list of over one hundred competencies said to characterize the autonomous learner. These characteristics are grouped under thirteen headings:

1. Be methodical and disciplined.
2. Be logical and analytical.
3. Be reflective and self-aware.
4. Demonstrate curiosity, openness, and motivation.
5. Be flexible.
6. Be interdependent and interpersonally competent.
7. Be persistent and responsible.
8. Be venturesome and creative.
9. Show confidence and have a positive self-concept.
10. Be independent and self-sufficient.
11. Have developed information seeking and retrieval skills.
12. Have knowledge about, and skill at, learning generally.
13. Develop and use defensible criteria for evaluating learning.

Approaches such as those of Knowles, and those of the authors surveyed by Candy, have been justly criticized for being too technical, and ignoring the social and political dimensions of learning. This view is expressed by Brookfield when he says it is "possible to be a superb technician of self-directed learning in terms of one's command of goal setting, instructional design or evaluative procedures, and yet to exercise no critical questioning of the validity or worth of one's intellectual pursuit" (1985, p. 29). Thus, while many of these characteristics may be acquired independently of context or subject matter, their possesion is not sufficient for autonomous learning. Perhaps a more complete version of the autonomous learner can be found in De Corte (1990), who identifies four categories of skills that a competent learner should possess:

1. Flexible application of a well-organised, domain specific knowledge base, involving concepts, rules, principles, formulas, and algorithms.

2. Heuristic methods, that is, systematic search strategies for problem analysis and transformation, such as carefully analysing a problem specifying the knowns and the unknowns; decomposing the problem into sub-goals; visualising the problem using a diagram or drawing.

3. Metacognitive skills, involving knowledge concerning one's own cognitive functioning, and activities that relate to the self-monitoring and regulation of one's cognitive processes, such as planning a solution process, and reflecting on one's learning and thinking activities.

4. Learning strategies, that is, activities that learners engage in during learning in order to acquire any of the three preceding types of skills [p. 92].

De Corte emphasizes the importance of domain-specific knowledge and the aquisition of learning skills pertinent to a particular domain. Others now acknowledge that autonomous learning is not a general, content-free capacity, and that it only makes sense in relation to a particular subject or domain of inquiry. Smith (1992), long a proponent of the learning-how-to-learn concept, acknowledges: "Recent research has confirmed that context impacts learning to learn more than was formerly apparent and precludes the possibility of providing people with generic training that yields adequate understandings and strategies for all occasions of learning and, of course, all life stages" (p. 175). Candy makes a similar assessment: "Nearly always, when we speak or write about learner self-direction, a degree of expertise of subject matter competence is also implied; we do not simply want people who can find resources for themselves, manage their time appropriately, or set learning goals, but rather learners who know and understand enough to be able to distinguish plausible from implausible knowledge claims or convincing from unconvincing evidence" (Candy, 1991, p. 344).

For those who stress subject-matter autonomy rather than general autonomy as a learner, the hallmark of the autonomous learner is the person who has developed a critical capacity in a particular subject area. Furthermore, this capacity must be nurtured as the learner comes to grips with the subject.

From a teaching point of view, the issue is how to approach a subject in a way that will enhance the learner's capacity to think independently in that subject. To this end, it is important to provide a framework that orients learners to the literature, to the methods of the discipline, and its conceptual tools, to the problems and issues posed, and to the state of knowledge in the discipline. Also, learners need to have an understanding of the historical development of the subject and the controversies within it. Fostering the spirit and capacity for critical inquiry requires a balance of expert input on substantive content, modeling of the critical thought process, and guidance of learners in developing their capacity to understand and analyze the subject matter. This version of promoting autonomy in relation to subject matter is teacher centered in the same way that we saw was the case for Kitchener and King. It too is at odds with the concept of learning through reflecting on experience, which Usher and others identify with the development of autonomous learning.

This apparent conflict can be understood by distinguishing between two forms of knowledge: the public and the private. Public knowledge is codified, it is consensually validated, and there are agreed procedures for judging knowledge claims. Disciplinary knowledge falls into this category, and it is largely this type of knowledge that is referred to by the phrase "subject matter autonomy." Private knowledge, in contrast, is tacit and highly situation-specific, much like the kinds of knowledge referred to when talking about practical intelligence and expertise. Many of the techniques in adult education that aim to foster the development of critical reflection on experience are directed at this second form of knowledge, the private.

Limits to the Autonomous Self

Given the nature of our society and the socialization process, what are the limits of personal autonomy? Is it desirable to point to personal autonomy as an ideal outcome of education and development?

These questions bring us back to a theme introduced in Chapter Five, the extent to which the self can be said to be socially constituted. Any view of the self as socially constituted imposes a limit on the capacity for personal autonomy. Usher (1992) quite rightly draws our attention to the way adult education, supported by the discipline of psychology, constructs the adult learner as an active meaning-giving subject, who, through self-consciousness, is both the source and shaper of experience. He writes, "The humanistic theorization of subjectivity posits an essential inner core—a true self unique to each individual, which is permanent, coherent and known to the individual. This true self may not always manifest itself fully because of the influence of psychological and social inhibitions which temporarily distort it and impede its full realization. Yet, despite these vicissitudes, the true self is always there and always present to itself. As a rational, unified center it can experience the world, including itself, and construct knowledge about the world and itself" (p. 202).

He is referring here to the individualism that, he claims, pervades thinking in humanistic adult education. The core ideas in the ethic of individualism are described by Lukes (1973): the belief in the supreme value and dignity of the individual; the idea of the individual as independent and autonomous, with thoughts and actions not determined by external agencies; and the idea of self-development, placing the onus on the individual to develop his or her talents to the fullest. This is a fair description of the ethic that has informed much of the adult education literature. But there is a growing opposition to this view, one which, in its extreme form, portrays the individual as merely an expression of distorting ideologies and oppressive social structures. Usher is mindful of this reaction, and warns that it is equally mistaken to adopt an over-socialized and over-determined view of the person: "Critical pedagogy . . . constructs another kind of subject, the exploited subject of 'false consciousness' whose experience is rendered inauthentic by distorting ideology and oppressive social structures. . . . As a consequence it tends to deprive subjects of agency by making them social victims" (1992, p. 203).

Thus he describes the two poles of the individual social dialectic, the psychological-humanistic pole asserting the agency of the subject, and the sociological pole asserting that the subject is wholly determined. The dilemma for the adult educator is that neither pole offers a satisfactory perspective on practice. The former seems too naive, in failing to acknowledge the power of social forces, and the latter is too pessimistic and leaves no scope for education to have a meaningful role—and no role for the autonomous learner.

Usher offers a way out of this dilemma. He urges us to embrace a postmodern perspective, and through it, a new engagement with the humanistic tradition. By a postmodern perspective, Usher means a focusing on language, text, and discourse as the means through which we analyze and understand our experiences and thereby construct ourselves. He writes, "We can only be the agents of our experience by engaging in a hermeneutic dialogue with the confused and often contradictory text of our experience of the world and of ourselves. The dialogue is one where formation in intersubjectivity and language, location in discourses and practical involvement in the world is a condition for the achievement of autonomy rather than a barrier to its discovery. Language, for example, does not merely constrain subjectivity but offers the possibility for constructing a critical self and social awareness through which subjectivity can be changed" (1992, p. 210).

Thus it is not the true or authentic self that is discovered through reflection on experience. Instead, experience is viewed as a text to be reinterpreted and reassessed. In effect, we learn to read the text into which our self has been inscribed, and we discover that there are alternative readings and therefore alternative selves to be constructed. This doesn't mean we can ascribe any meaning to our experiences or that we can create any self we choose. We need to give a plausible reading to our experience, one that can legitimately contest more obvious interpretations. Also, the self remains situated in history and culture and continually open to reinscription and reformulation. The autonomous self is thus neither an end state nor something standing outside history and culture. The autonomous self recognizes its situatedness and its limits and possibilities of reinterpretation and reformation.

Brookfield (1993) has also addressed the tension between the humanistic concepts of autonomy and self-direction and the opposing, more critical concepts of ideology and oppression. He argues that there is a need to reassert the political dimensions of self-direction. He begins by summarizing the position of writers such as Griffin (1983, 1987) and Collins (1991), who portray humanistic adult educators as being overly accommodative, depoliticizing and decontextualizing adult education practice into a concern with techniques for promoting personal growth. While Brookfield acknowledges that this is indeed a problem for adult education, he denies that self-direction and autonomy are necessarily accommodative, noncritical, and nonemancipatory concepts. He argues that self-direction is in fact inherently political in that genuine self-directed learning shifts control from the institution to the learner. Providing the conditions that self-direction requires, such as access to resources, exposes and challenges institutional decision-making processes. Even though he is approaching the issue from a very different direction from that of Usher, his solution is remarkably similar:

> The self in a self directed learning project is not an autonomous, innocent self, contentedly floating free from cultural influences. It has not sprung fully formed out of a political vacuum. It is, rather, an embedded self, a self whose instincts, values, needs and beliefs have been shaped by the surrounding culture. As such, it is a self that reflects the constraints and contradictions, as well as the liberatory possibilities, of that culture. The most critically sophisticated and reflective adults cannot escape their own biographies . . . an important aspect of a fully adult self-directed learning project should be a reflective awareness how one's desires and needs have been culturally formed [1993, p. 236].

It is reassuring that both Usher and Brookfield come to the same broad conclusion, that although individuals cannot transcend or eradicate their historical and cultural situatedness (and neither should they, necessarily), there is nevertheless room to maneuver in the continuing interplay of self and others—and it is in this space that autonomy resides.

Strategies for Promoting Personal Autonomy

What does this view of autonomy and self-direction mean for adult educators committed to developing autonomy among their students? The literature presents some techniques and approaches that can enhance adult education practice. Three tools in particular are well worth considering: Freire's "culture circle" (1974), Deshler's "metaphor analysis" (1991), and Peters's "action-reason-thematic" technique (1991). Keep in mind, however, that technique alone will not guarantee that students always develop the type of autonomy we have been discussing.

Freire originally used the idea of a culture circle while developing literacy programs in Brazil in the early 1960s. He was interested in fostering a more critical awareness among the learners. In particular, he was interested in helping the learners become aware of their own agency, and realize that they could both reflect on and act in the world. The first step toward this, he argues, is to appreciate the distinction between the world of nature (which exists on its own terms regardless of human action) and the world of culture (which is a human creation and thereby alterable). The culture circle works through a coordinator initiating a dialogue on nature and culture by using the vocabulary, themes, and agendas of the learners. Typical situations are represented pictorially, as in the three sketches shown in Figure 6.1. Each sketch depicts a situation to be decoded by the participants as a group, with the help of the coordinator.

Freire reports the words of one participant who comments on all three sketches: " 'Of these three, only two are hunters—the two men. They are hunters because they make culture before and after they hunt' (He failed only to say that they made culture while they hunted). 'The third, the cat, does not make culture, either before or after the hunt. He is not a hunter he is a pursuer' " (1974, p. 71).

By making this subtle distinction between hunting and pursuing, this man grasped the fundamental point: the creation of culture. The point is that once the learners appreciate the distinction between nature and culture they then see the possibility of challenging previously taken-for-granted aspects of everyday life. Problems such as housing, clothing, diet, health, education, and so on are now seen as problems that can be transformed through political action.

The metaphor analysis approach, described by Deshler (1991) has elements in common with Freire's approach. Here are the eight steps Deshler defines for the process:

1. Select a primary subject from the three domains described above (personal, popular culture, and organization domains).

2. Scan their memories associated with the primary subject and try to recognize several metaphors that were or are in use with that

Figure 6.1. Ilustrations Used in Culture Circles.

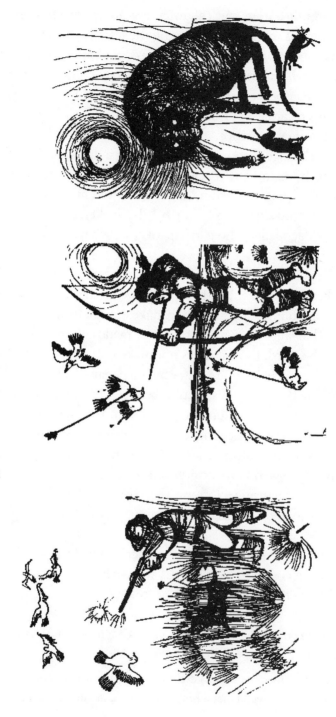

Source: Freire, 1974, pp. 66, 68, 70. Reprinted by permission.

primary subject. If they cannot think of any easily, then ask them to create metaphors that describe their past experience with that primary subject. (A few people may have difficulty at first. Without trying to influence their memory or their selection or creation, several metaphors that others have used may be provided as examples.)

3. Select one of the metaphors they have recognized or created. Ask them to take that metaphor and unpack it by describing in detail on paper its meaning in reference to the primary subject. (If this is being done in a large group, learners could be encouraged to share their metaphors and unpacked meanings with others in groups of two or three people. When unpacking the meaning perspective of a metaphor, learners can ask themselves what characteristics of the metaphor correspond to each of the unexamined realities under consideration and what examples from memory illustrate each characteristic.)

4. Reflect on the values, beliefs, and assumptions that are embedded in the meanings of the metaphors.

5. Question the validity of each metaphor's meanings by comparing these with their own life experience, knowledge, information, and values or belief systems that confirm or deny the meanings derived from the metaphors. Ask themselves if they now affirm these same assumptions, beliefs, values, or understandings.

6. Create new metaphors that express meanings that they now want to emphasize regarding the primary subject under discussion. Share those meanings with others and listen to what others are creating and expressing.

7. Consider implications for action that derive from the newly created metaphor.

8. Repeat the process with additional metaphors for the same primary subject or go on to new primary subjects in the personal, popular culture, or organization domains [pp. 299–300].

Learners are encouraged to develop metaphors from material in one of three domains: the personal domain (relating to family lifestyle, parents and parenting, careers, gender and human sexuality, sports and leisure activities, financial resources); the popular culture domain (products, vehicles, art and architecture, popular music and literature); and the organizational domain (educational institutions, places of employment, religious institutions, government, social movements). For example, metaphors to describe childhood family lifestyle may be cafeteria, nest, baseball game, circus, or prison. The aim is to discuss the meaning of the metaphor, to create new meanings and new metaphors to represent one's experiences more effectively, and to clarify one's world view. Deshler insists that learners need to collaborate in this task (best in triads and dyads) and that they should clearly understand its purpose.

The Peters action-reason-thematic technique (1991) is an interview technique that aims to unmask the network of assumptions governing our approach to a problem. The technique involves five steps:

1. Identification and definition of the interviewee's problem
2. Establishment of the time frame of the problem, tracing its history and course to date
3. Identification and description of specific actions taken to solve the problem
4. Identification and description of reasons for each action taken
5. Reduction of actions and reasons to argument themes, which the interviewer extracts from the text of the interview

It is this last stage that makes Peters's approach similar to the other two approaches described. During this stage, the analysis becomes increasingly couched in terms of the interviewer's language and interpretations. Peters illustrates his approach with reference to a mother who is unable to read or write and whose nine-year-old daughter suffers from a vision problem. The following is a condensed version of this case study, based on Peters, 1991, pp. 326–330.

Actions taken

1. I talked with Tora.
2. I talked with Tora's father.
3. I decided Tora didn't need glasses.
4. I talked with Tora's teacher.
5. I talked with my sister.
6. I talked with a nurse.
7. I took Tora to an eye doctor.
8. I became very upset.
9. I made an appointment to get Tora glasses.

Sample of reasons for actions

1. Action 2

   I ask my husband about things I don't understand.

   I wanted to know what he thought was wrong.

2. Action 3

   Her father said she didn't need glasses because her eyes weren't crossed.

3. Action 5

   I talk to my sister about things.

   One of her daughters has a vision problem.

   She ought to know what is going on.

   She told me that something was wrong with Tora's eyes.

   I thought she would know what to do.

   Reasons advanced for her propensity to ask others

If someone is not very smart, it pays to ask someone who is. I don't have an education.

1. Someone in the family has to be in charge. I think my husband is in this family.

2. My sister was always the smart one when we were growing up. I've always looked up to her.

3. Doctors are supposed to know. Don't they?

Interpretation

> Lillie's assumptions and characterization of these significant people in her life suggest some more basic assumptions about authority and the protector roles that others play in her life. In the case of Tora's vision problems, she relied on some sense of authority that she assigned to these people, even to the point of rejecting the meaning of her own direct experience with the problem, these assumptions and perhaps others lie at a deeper structure in Lillie's thinking and seem worthy of further discussion.

Note that it is the interviewer who provides the interpretation. This interpretation, which must be consistent with the interviewee's life world, is then used as the basis for discussion with the interviewee to identify further assumptions.

All three of the above techniques have the potential to promote the kind of situated autonomy discussed earlier. They must, however, be appropriate to the learning context. In the case of the culture circle, autonomy and critical thinking are linked to the task of learning to read and write. The metaphor analysis is aimed directly at enhancing personal autonomy without reference to a particular context. The action-reason-thematic technique is used where there is an identifiable problem the learner wishes to address. Although these techniques do not apply in all contexts, there are some common features that can guide the further development of similar techniques suited to different contexts. They all stress the central role of dialogue and the identification and exploration of the meanings that learners attach to events and situations. They all have a concrete starting point around which the dialogue takes place: a drawing, a metaphor, or a problem. And they all require the assistance of others in exploring meanings, whether for sharing ideas, offering interpretations, or posing questions.

The challenge for adult educators is to promote situated autonomy in the context of their own work. This of course takes a great deal of inventiveness and skill, and above all, presupposes a critical approach to one's own area of expertise. It is possible to reformulate existing teaching techniques to allow for the development of situated autonomy. This can be illustrated with reference to Knowles's learning contract method. The common format used for learning contracts could be reformulated to avoid the charge that they are accommodating and promote conformity to established interests. For example, the original format proposed by Knowles (Exhibit 6.1) could be recast to give it a more critical edge.

In Knowles's view, the learning objectives are derived from a diagnosis of learning needs: "A learning need is the gap between where you are now and where you want to be in regard to a particular set of competencies" (1978, p. 233). Knowles's definition of a learning need assumes that some deficiency exists in the learner and that this deficiency can be remedied through the acquisition of specifiable competencies. This has been criticized for being an overly instrumentalist and accommodative approach. As such, neither of these assumptions would be satisfactory as starting points for a more critical approach. A more critical approach would seek to problematize the identification of needs much more than the instrumentalist approach. The facilitator's role is to assist learners to articulate their real learning needs—not to uncritically accept their statements of wants and desires. Also, the articulation of needs will not necessarily lead to unambiguous objectives. In a critical approach, the first column in the learning contract may therefore contain a statement of the issue, problem, or concern under investigation. Questions posed in this column would include: For whom is there a concern or issue? Whose interests are being served by addressing the issue? Who shares your concern? Do others have a

Exhibit 6.1. A Typical Learning Contract.

Learning Contracts for:

Name _____

Activity _____

Learning Objectives	Learning Resources and Strategies	Evidence of Accomplishment of Objectives	Criteria and Means for Validating Evidence

Source: From *The Adult Learner: A Neglected Species*, by Malcolm Knowles. Copyright © 1978 by Gulf Publishing Company, Houston, TX. Used with permission. All rights reserved.

different perspective on the issue? What do you wish to learn and how does this address the issue? Some questions (in addition to those proposed by Knowles) under the second column "Learning Resources and Strategies" may include: Where is the relevant knowledge and information? Is it accessible? If not, what can be done to make it accessible? Do the strategies you propose privilege the perspective of one group over another? Do you need to explore other perspectives? The final two columns will need to be stated in a tentative way, principally because learning outcomes will be more uncertain with a critical approach. This is because such an approach employs dialogue and questioning as a basic tool, and learning needs may become transformed in the process. The third column, "Evidence of Accomplishment of Objectives," may be better worded as "Evidence of Learning Outcomes."

Conclusion

This chapter began by outlining some basic types of autonomy, such as intellectual, moral, and emotional. We pointed out the differences between autonomy in the context of education and autonomy as a general personal attribute. Then we explored the link between personal autonomy and learner autonomy, surveying the literature on the development of personal autonomy for associations with attitudes and conceptions of education and learning. In this context, we addressed the issue of whether autonomous and self-directed learning is a general or domain-specific attribute, and discussed some of the limits to personal autonomy, given that autonomy makes sense only in a social context. This line of reasoning led to the conclusion that adult educators need to approach teaching and learning in a way that promotes the development of situated autonomy among their students. Subsequent chapters turn to the subject of helping students capitalize on their own experience to enhance the learning process.

Chapter Seven

Adult Education and the Reconstruction of Experience

The importance and centrality of experience as a foundation for adult education practice is widely accepted. This is so for a number of reasons. Kolb (1984), for example, points to some trends in higher education which have prompted the idea that the experiences of learners should be acknowledged. There are growing numbers of nontraditional students in higher education, for whom formal academic approaches are inappropriate. They have, it is argued, a more "street-wise" or practical approach to learning, and experiential methods allow them to capitalize on their experience. Likewise, growing numbers of mature adults starting or returning to higher education have confronted educators with students who scrutinize ideas and knowledge in terms of accumulated life experiences and not solely in terms of conceptual clarity, internal consistency, fit with experimental observation, and other academic criteria. In addition, the movement toward vocationalism in higher education has been accompanied by a demand for stronger links between education and work, and experiential learning methods help educators to address this demand. Finally, there is pressure for higher education institutions to develop strategies for assessing prior work and life experiences for the purpose of granting academic credit or certification.

Other reasons for the emphasis on experience in adult education can be traced to the acceptance of certain views about the nature of learning and the teacher-learner relationship. Focusing on the learner's experience is an integral part of the tradition that places the learner at the center of the education process. Both

Dewey (1963) and Freire (1972), in their own ways, have contrasted highly formal, subject-centered and teacher-centered educational methods with those that take the experience of learners as a point of departure. The aim is to develop active, self-aware learners who have the capacity and freedom to frame their own purposes. Received concepts in adult education, such as andragogy, self-directed learning, autonomy, and critical reflection, are based on sentiments similar to those expressed by Dewey and Freire.

The justification for learning based on experience can also be found in the psychological literature. In cognitive psychology, Piaget (1978) and Bruner (1973) have stressed the interactive nature of the relationship between learning and experience. Learning is an active process in the sense that learners are continually trying to understand and make sense of their experiences. In effect, learners reconstruct their experiences to match more closely their existing rules and categories for understanding the world. These rules and categories may also change to accommodate new experiences. From another perspective, the psychodynamic psychologies draw attention to the emotionally laden nature of the relationship between experience and learning. In this regard, the work of Rogers (1951) and Maslow (1968) has had a substantial impact on adult education. In particular, their emphasis on personal freedom, choice, and the validity of subjective experience can be seen in the importance adult educators attach to the concept of self in learning.

In the adult education literature from Gibb (1960) and McClusky (1964) to Brookfield (1987) and Jarvis (1987a, 1987b), experience is consistently cited as a distinguishing characteristic of adult learning. But what does it mean for an adult educator to acknowledge the experiences of learners? Clearly, there are different ways in which experience can be acknowledged. First, at the most basic or superficial level teachers can link their explanations and illustrations to the prior experiences of learners. By doing so, they build a bridge from the known to the unknown. Second, teachers can attempt to link learning activities to current experiences at work, home, or in the community. This is typically done by adapting material to the immediate problems and concerns of learners, thereby ensuring that learning is relevant. A third possibility is to create experiences such as simulations, games, and role plays, from which learning will flow as a result of the active participation of the learners. Such activities establish a common experience base for the students, who can then construct meaning through personal reflection and group discussion. Finally, experience can be used as the primary source for learning. Typically the meanings that learners attach to their experiences are subjected to critical scrutiny through the medium of the group. The adult educator may consciously set out to disrupt the learner's world view and stimulate uncertainty, ambiguity, and doubt about previously taken-for-granted interpretations of experience—new interpretations emerging from this exercise.

In each of the above strategies, learners' experiences are treated quite differently, but there is a common supposition that education must somehow stimulate learners to go beyond their experiences. It can safely be said that learning involves more than the mere confirmation of experience. Indeed, experience has to be mediated and reconstructed (or transformed) by the student for learning to occur. A crucial issue is how and under what conditions people can reconstruct their experiences and thereby learn.

For the adult educator, the principal tension is between the experiences of the learners in a particular domain and the codified knowledge of that domain, as represented in theory and research reported in books and journals. This tension can also be described as between individual subjective experience and collective experience of a situation. The four approaches to experience identified above represent different ways of addressing this tension, and as such they form a useful framework for further exploring it.

Linking Material to Prior Experiences

It has long been recognized that learners can only make sense of new material in terms of their prior learning and experience. Good teachers illustrate their material by constantly referring to the learners' prior experiences. Of course, teachers can never really know the experiences of all their students, or for that matter know all the experiences of even a single student. There are two issues for the teacher: how to get to know the students' experiences and then how to make appropriate links with the material.

There are several ways for teachers to become familiar with students' prior experiences. For example, they can test the students' knowledge formally or informally, conduct individual interviews, distribute precourse questionnaires, invite open-ended submissions, call for detailed curricula vitae, arrange precourse work visits, require a statement of prior experience, and so on. Information about prior experiences can also be evoked during the class through group discussion, questioning, set exercises, and other methods requiring student participation. Experienced teachers tend to develop a conception of the "typical" student and adjust their explanations and illustrations to fit this conception. This becomes problematic when a teacher's assumptions are inappropriate for all or some of the students. There is a particular need to be sensitive to lifestyle, cultural, and gender differences here. Casual references to television shows, sporting events, family living, social issues, current affairs, and recreational pursuits are part of the normal fare for most teachers—but the assumption that the students share the teacher's interests can be dangerous, and the assumption that the students naturally adopt the same position as the teacher is even worse. The authors have seen teachers assume that students are married, or are heterosexual, or enjoy a particular sport such as football, or have parents and children, or have material possessions such as a home, car, or computer. In general, these teachers were quite dumbfounded when they alienated or angered students with their "harmless" casual comments. When students' experiences are unknown, references to them should be at least tentative or provisional—and teachers need to be sensitive to the feedback they receive and to shift ground when it is called for.

Knowing something about students is an enormous asset for the teacher. It makes it possible to provide continuity between the material and the learners' experiences. New material can be related to prior experiences by pointing out similarities and differences, analogous relationships, new applications, logical extensions, and possible syntheses.

This level of acknowledging experience clearly uses experience to fulfill the teacher's purposes. Experience is seen as a conduit for effective learning, and as such it is a good but traditional educational practice. The purpose is to relate the present to the past, to ensure continuity in the acquisition of skill and knowledge.

This is what Dewey referred to as the principle of continuity: "Every experience is a moving force. Its value can be judged only on the ground of what it moves toward and into" (1963, p. 35) and later, "In a certain sense every experience should do something to prepare a person for later experiences of a deeper and more expansive quality. That is the very meaning of growth, continuity, reconstruction of experience" (1963, p. 47).

This idea of moving from the known to the unknown suggests an image of development that is continuous rather than discontinuous, and harmonious rather than based on conflict. But others argue that a sense of disjuncture and conflict are necessary for learning to occur. Indeed, many of the developmental theories described earlier suggest that conflict and disequilibrium are preconditions for development. This issue is identified by Jarvis as one of the paradoxes of learning: "Disjuncture occurs whenever there is lack of accord between the external world experienced by human beings and their internal biographical interests and knowledge. . . . Disjuncture makes learning possible. The paradox is that if harmony is fully established, there can be no learning situation" (Jarvis, 1992, p. 83).

If it is accepted that the striving for harmony and balance is the driving force for learning and development, then disjuncture is a necessary precondition for learning and development. The task for the teacher is to introduce new material in a way that links with—but at the same time challenges—learners' prior experiences. It should be noted here that, irrespective of the teacher's intent, learners will always attempt to link new material to their prior experiences. Perhaps the principal challenge for the teacher, then, is to understand how the learners are making sense of the material in terms of their prior experiences.

Relating Learning to Current Experiences

When current experiences are brought into play, the emphasis shifts from the continuity of learning and experience (the vertical dimension) to the interaction of learning with experience (the horizontal dimension). Once again, it is possible to locate this idea in the writing of Dewey: "Every experience enacted and undergone modifies the one who acts and undergoes, while this modification affects, whether we wish it or not, the quality of subsequent experiences" (1963, p. 35).

This is what Dewey refers to as the "principle of interaction," which he regards as indispensable for learning and growth. In its more crude form, it is the application of learning to experience. Instead of "How can I use my past experiences to make sense of this material?" the question becomes "How can I use this knowledge to make sense of my current experiences?" The concern with relevance and usefulness is normally the driving motive for linking current experiences to the material being learned. The danger of the utility motive is that a theory-to-practice attitude may dominate in areas where it is inappropriate. A theory-to-practice attitude is one where the theory is learned and then applied to practical situations at work, in the home, or in community life. This is appropriate with mechanical or procedural tasks, or where the theory is based on phenomena governed by immutable laws. Where this is not the case, it is more appropriate to consider theory *interacting* with practice. Collins (1991) addresses this issue in reference to the profession of adult education:

> Adult educators, along with other professionals, often suggest that competent performance is a matter of familiarizing oneself with theories and, then, of putting these acquired theories into practice as

relevant occasions arise. This does not seem to represent the case in any of the roles, professional or otherwise, we perform in our everyday world. "Putting theory into practice", as the problem is often characterized, carries with it the presumption that a particular theoretical model can faithfully represent a particular order of reality. This deterministic notion, questioned even in the natural sciences, is not at all appropriate for the human sciences, which focus on the problem of human performance (competence) and provide much of the knowledge base for the helping professions. Though an understanding of theoretical constructions is important to any serious vocational endeavour, it is more efficacious to think in terms of engaging thoughtfully with theory and, then, putting *ourselves* into practice rather than putting theory into practice [p. 47].

What is gained by this subtle shift from "theory into practice" to "ourselves into practice"? It moves the emphasis from knowledge being contained within formal theory to knowledge being created from practice. The implication is that theory can inform practice and that practice can inform theory. It is not a matter of asking whether theory, in the light of practice, is confirmed or disconfirmed. Instead, the question is whether theory helps to illuminate practice, whether it improves our potential as reflective practitioners and assists us to interpret and understand our practice: Does it provide us with a discourse for analyzing practice? Similarly, it is not appropriate to ask whether practice, in the light of theory, is good or bad. Judgments about the value of practice need to be made according to criteria that lie outside of theory.

For example, consider the relationship between theory and practice in music. In music, "theory" refers partly to the relationships between scales and between chords and partly to rules for resolving musical problems in different styles. It is possible to be an accomplished musician without a knowledge of theory as such, although the knowledge may be implicit. Likewise, people often make aesthetic judgments about music without regard to the niceties of theory. Music can be appreciated without any formal knowledge of theory or any practical experience. In addition, it is clearly possible to have a good grasp of theory without being particularly competent on any instrument. It is thus possible to have theoretical knowledge without practical expertise, practical expertise without theoretical knowledge, and musical appreciation without any explicit knowledge or expertise. Theory can enhance both appreciation and musical performance, but strictly speaking it is necessary for neither. Furthermore, the best music rarely conforms to the dictates of theory. This by no means devalues the important role of musical theory, which codifies and illuminates practice, and which provides a base for discourse, teaching, interpretation, and understanding.

Arguably, the same relation pertains between theory and practice for most of the tasks we are faced with in adult life. It is certainly true of the development of expertise in working life as discussed in Chapter Three. The task for the teacher is to build on the capacity for theory to enhance experience and for experience to enhance theory. This is particularly difficult for someone coming from a strong disciplinary background with its own internal logic and rational sequential development. Furthermore, any discipline by itself is rarely likely to be sufficient to inform current experience—experience does not respect disciplinary boundaries. If the discipline is seen as paramount, current experiences mainly serve to help understand the theory. If the link with experience is paramount, theoretical constructs mainly serve to illuminate current experiences. In the best scenario, the discipline is introduced in the context of shared experiences and both outcomes are achieved: theory illuminates practice and practice illuminates theory.

Creating New Experiences

Teachers can design group experiences where the experience itself becomes the focal point for learning (as distinct from the kind of experience that forms a part of all learning, which may be referred to as practice). Such focal-point activities include simulations, games, and role plays where the shared experience forms the raw data for learning in the group. Learning typically occurs through active participation in the experience and subsequent analysis of the experience. This comes much closer to the idea of *learning from experience* than the approaches considered above, which make use of prior or current experience from outside the class setting. Here experience is unequivocally preeminent. However, such planned experiences are often removed from the complexities of reality. They represent an attempt to mimic, condense, or provide an analogue of real-world experiences that the learners have yet to encounter. In such planned experiences, the essential elements of the real world are present, although often in an abstract or stylized way. For example, simulations are frequently used to help people prepare for interviews, deal with interpersonal conflict, or learn to manage committee meetings. They prepare participants for the kinds of issues and problems encountered, but they are not in themselves concrete instances in the lived experience of the learner. In some instances, they represent a reversal of the real-world order, for instance when parents "play" their children, husbands their wives, managers their employees, or when males play females—and vice versa. Some experiences are designed to be are self-contained and refer only to themselves. Ice-breaker exercises illustrate this; their whole point is for participants to "experience each other" and thus lay the foundation for subsequent learning in the group. Games are also used in this way. For example, teachers of management and other forms of organized behavior often employ games that appear at first to promote competition but are actually best solved through cooperation. Such games highlight the qualities that participants bring to the learning group—indeed they often function like moral parables.

Learning experiences like those described above often produce unexpected outcomes. The rules are set up to motivate participation and interaction, but the actual dynamics of this interaction are unpredictable. The exercise is judged to be successful if sufficient interaction occurs so that analysis can follow. But are all outcomes equally instructive? If not, then how can teachers ensure that experiences are not negative from an educational point of view? Is the postexperience analysis (often called debriefing) sufficient to guard against negative outcomes? Dewey has the following to say on this matter:

> The belief that all genuine education comes about through experience does not mean that all experiences are genuinely or equally educative. Experience and education cannot be directly equated to each other. For some experiences are mis-educative. Any experience is mis-educative that has the effect of arresting or distorting the growth of further experience. An experience may be such as to engender callousness; it may produce lack of sensitivity and of responsiveness. Then the possibilities of having richer experience in the future are restricted. . . . Again, experiences may be so disconnected from one another that, while each is agreeable or even exciting in itself, they are not linked cumulatively to one another. Energy is then dissipated and a person becomes scatter-brained. Each experience may be lively, vivid, and "interesting", and yet their disconnectedness may artificially generate dispersive, disintegrated, centrifugal habits. The consequence of formation of such habits is inability to control future experiences. . . . Everything depends upon the quality of the experience which is had. The quality of any experience has two aspects. There is an immediate aspect of agreeableness or disagreeableness, and there is its influence upon later experiences. The first is obvious and easy to judge. The effect of an experience is not borne on its face. It sets a problem to the educator. It is his business to arrange for the kind of experiences which, while they do not repel the student, but rather engage his or her activities are, nevertheless, more than immediately enjoyable since they promote having desirable future experiences. Just as no man or woman lives or dies to himself or herself, so no experience lives and dies to itself. Wholly independent of desire or intent, every experience lives on in further experiences. Hence the central problem of an education based upon experience is to select the kind of present

experiences that live fruitfully and creatively in subsequent experiences [pp. 25–27].

Dewey was writing here about educational experiences in general, but his views are particularly relevant to those who design structured experiences like those under discussion. The design and conduct of a structured experience for learning requires substantial creativity and managerial skill. Structured learning experiences are generally psychologically charged, and require careful monitoring.

Role plays and simulations, for example, require participants to explore prescribed roles. In playing out a scenario, participants project their own thoughts and feelings into the script (unless, of course, they are accomplished actors). In a sense, it is self-exploration through the mask of the other—which may be more revealing and threatening than direct methods of self-examination. In addition, structured learning experiences are invariably conducted in small groups and participants are subject to the pressures of group norms, which means they are more likely to be compliant than might otherwise be the case. The power of group norms is well documented in the social psychological literature.

One well-known example of research using a simulation technique is Zimbardo's prison simulation (1976). Zimbardo, a psychologist working at Stanford University, was interested in reproducing the essential elements of the prison environment. Students were allocated randomly to play the roles of guards and prisoners. Zimbardo went to great lengths to make the simulation realistic—students were arrested at home, prisoners were referred to only by number, prison cells were located in a basement of the university, and so on. The simulation had to be abandoned before its scheduled completion, principally because the participants were becoming enmeshed in their roles to the extent that considerable resentment, anxiety, and conflict were emerging. The Zimbardo experiment is a powerful illustration of the force of simulated group activities on those who participate.

Learning from Experience

The use of lived (rather than created) experience as the primary source for learning seems to be a general feature of education aiming at social justice and/or personal transformation. It is also increasingly becoming a feature of continuing professional education, which may also include personal transformation within its scope. This approach to learning from experience can be stated quite simply:

The first task is get people to talk about their experiences.

The second task is to analyze those experiences individually or collectively.

The third task is to identify and act on the implications of what is revealed.

This basic framework has inspired a number of well-documented approaches, all concerned with promoting reflection on experience. We have already commented on the work of Mezirow and Freire, and on metaphor analysis and the action-reason-thematic technique. Some further approaches to reflection on experience are described below.

Donald Schön's seminal works, *The Reflective Practitioner* (1983) and *Educating the Reflective Practitioner* (1987), have as their genesis a realization that there is a "crisis of confidence in the professions" (1983, p. 4). Further, "Professionally designed solutions to public problems have had unanticipated consequences, sometimes worse than the problems they were designed to solve" (1983, p. 4). Far from improving our lot, Schön notes, increasing specialization and reliance on the "hard" knowledge of science and scholarship over the "soft" knowledge of artistry and unvarnished opinion no longer provide solutions to the complex and intractable problems we face. It is at this point that Schön's interest in learning from experience expresses itself. As a solution to the scenario outlined, he advocates what he terms "reflection-in-action," the process by which he sees professionals engaging with problems and learning experientially. That is, reflecting on experience in the midst of practice.

He writes: "Practitioners themselves often reveal a capacity for reflection on their intuitive knowing in the midst of action and sometimes use this capacity to cope with the unique, uncertain and conflicting situations of practice" (1983, pp. viii–ix). Schön thus emphasizes that learning from experience takes place through reflecting in the process of experience, and that this often happens at an intuitive, tacit level.

In comparison, David Boud and associates (Boud, Keogh, and Walker, 1985a; Boud and Walker, 1991, 1990, 1992; Boud, 1992) initially differed from Schön's understanding. They emphasized reflection *after* the event as the key factor in promoting learning from experience. Boud and Walker (1992) explored the relationship between themselves and Schön: "There is a fundamental tension between becoming fully immersed in an event and standing back to witness our own actions. The former is required if we are to be a full player in the event, the latter is implicit in the conception of reflection" (p. 167). Of their first conception of a learning experience, they wrote, "[there are] two main components [of an experience]: the experience and then reflective activity based on that experience" (Boud, Keogh, and Walker, 1985b, p. 18).

After acknowledging criticism of their initial model on the basis that it gave little credence to the totality of life experiences the learner brought to any single learning experience, they subsequently revised their views to "encompass reflection in the midst of experience and the foundations on which learning builds" (Boud and Walker, 1992, p. 168). This latter stance aligns them more closely with Schön, as they came to believe that "we experience as we reflect, and we reflect as we experience" (Boud and Walker, 1992, p. 167). Thus, their most recent model of learning through experience (seen in Figure 7.1) accounts for the preparation the learner brings to the experience, the experience itself (during which the learner can both "notice" and "intervene"), and the two-way process of reflecting back and forward during and subsequent to the experience.

Figure 7.1 Learning from Experience.

Milieu

Focus on:
Learner
Milieu
Skills/
Strategies

Noticing   Reflection   Intervening
in Action

Personal
Foundation
of
Exerience

Intent

Return to
Experience
Attend to Feelings
Re-evaluate the
Experience

Preparation   Experience   Reflective Processes

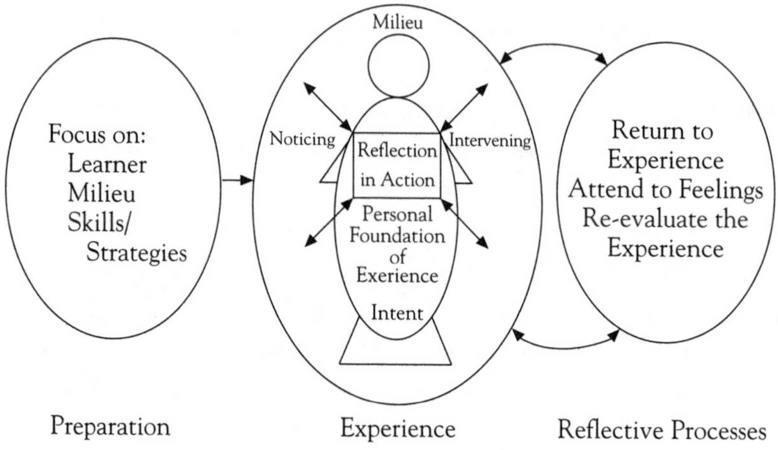

Source: From Boud and Walker, 1990, p. 67 (see also Boud and Walker, 1992).

Others have also shown an interest in the process of learning from experience. Evans (1990, 1992) and Simosko (1991), for example, are among those who seek to chart and legitimize learning from experience in pursuit of the Recognition of Prior Learning, otherwise known as Accreditation of Prior Learning, or Prior Learning Assessment. Evans writes, "Experience of life, leisure and work may be a rich source of learning but there is no prescribed curriculum and no certification to prove it" (1990, p. 122).

She agrees with Schön and Boud that reflection is the key to learning from experience (Evans, 1992, pp. 87–88) and that all experience is not necessarily learning. Senge, a systems theorist, notes similarly that in the business world "the most powerful learning comes from experience" (1990, p. 23).

Brookfield (1991, p. 177) regards critical reflection as the key to learning from experience. This involves three phases:

1. The identification of the assumptions that underlie thoughts and actions

2. The scrutiny of the accuracy and validity of these assumptions in terms of how they connect to experience

3. The reconstituting of these assumptions to make them more inclusive and integrative

The recognition and analysis of assumptions is the key to critical reflection. In the critical incident approach, "learners are asked to produce richly detailed accounts of specific events and then move to a collaborative, inductive analysis of general elements embedded in these particular descriptions" (1991, p. 181). Brookfield describes three examples of critical incident exercises he has devised. They all follow the same pattern: the participants are asked to describe a concrete event that has triggered an emotional response, guided by questions like when? where? who was involved? and so forth. Then follows further guidance on how to proceed, which is standardized for all three exercises:

Now, find two other participants to form a group of three. In this triad, each person will take a turn reading aloud his or her description. After you have read out your description, your two colleagues will try to identify the assumptions about good educational practice that they think are embedded in your description. You, in turn, will do the same for each of your colleagues. To help you identify assumptions, it might be helpful to think of them as the rules of thumb that underlie and inform our actions. In this exercise, they are the general beliefs, commonsense ideas, or intuitions that you and your colleagues hold about teaching.

Your analysis of assumptions should initially be on two levels: (1) What assumptions do you think inform your colleagues' choices of significant incidents—what do their choices say about their value systems? (2) What assumptions underlie the specific actions they took in the incidents described? After your description has been analyzed by your two colleagues, you have the opportunity to comment on what you see as the accuracy and validity of their insights. Do you think they have gauged accurately the assumptions you hold?

Were you surprised by their analyses? Or did the assumptions they identify confirm how you see your own practice? They, in turn, will have the chance to comment on the accuracy and validity of your assessments of their assumptions.

It is also interesting to look for commonalities and differences in the assumptions you each identify. If there are commonly held assumptions, do they represent what passes for conventional wisdom in your field of practice? If there are major differences, to what extent might these signify divergent views in the field at large? Or might the differences be the result of contextual variations? [1991, pp. 182–183]

This exercise concludes with a group analysis of assumptions. The general features of the exercise are that

1. The focus is on the learners' experiences (those that are emotionally significant).
2. Learners work from the specific to the general.
3. There is an emphasis on peer learning.
4. Assumptions from conventional wisdom are analyzed.
5. There is a debriefing of the form and focus of the exercise.

It is useful to compare and contrast these general features with the principles identified by Hart in her companion article, "Liberation Through Consciousness Raising" (1990):

1. Use personal experience as the original source of material for critical reflection.
2. Assemble a group with common experiences and assumptions. Maintain equality among all participants in the group.
3. Acknowledge the existence of power and oppression.
4. Gain and sustain a theoretical distance from the material.

Although her purpose is more clearly targeted toward women as an oppressed group—and she warns against applying her principles without regard to context—there are some commonalities with Brookfield in the principles she espouses. They both regard personal experience as the source of learning, and they are both concerned with unmasking power relations and how they operate (this is implicit in Brookfield's requirement to analyze the assumptions of conventional wisdom). They are also both concerned with moving beyond the specific experiences of individual participants to the construction of more general concepts, ideas, or theories to link these experiences within and beyond the group (Hart's "theoretical distance"), and finally they share the use of peer reflection and critique and an implied or explicit equality among those peers.

Perhaps the most significant feature of the above approaches (and others like them) is that there is a clear requirement to move beyond the exploration of personal meaning. Thus the attribution of meaning to experience cannot simply be a personal, unique, and private enterprise conducted without reference to existing bodies of knowledge or to the experiences of others. This point, of course, was well made by Dewey (1963) in his discussion of the relation between objective and subjective knowledge. For him, knowledge is the product of an interaction between the experiencing subject and the external objective world. The previous chapter referred to Usher's view that the self is the product of social forces and is thus not fixed, rational, and always present to itself. "Meanings, and therefore the meaning of experience, is not guaranteed by subjectivity because the latter is itself constituted in language. This implies that although experience belongs to us as individual subjects, we are not the authors of the meaning of our experience" (1989, p. 29).

The approaches to critical reflection described above acknowledge that we are not the sole authors of the meaning of our experience. On the other hand, although the meanings one attributes to experience are influenced by language, history, and culture, they are not wholly determined, or, more to the point, they are not permanently fixed. Language, history, and culture can themselves become the object of critical inquiry. This is precisely the strategy adopted by those adult educators who, first and foremost, aim to challenge the meanings attributed to experiences among the groups with which they work.

A classic psychological experiment on obedience illustrates some of the above ideas and their complexity. The researcher in question, Milgram (1965), was interested in documenting the extent to which people would carry out the instructions of an authority figure, even when those instructions violated strongly held beliefs. Here is Milgram's description of the essential elements of the study:

> The focus of the study concerns the amount of electric shock a subject is willing to administer to another person when ordered by an experimenter to give the "victim" increasingly more severe punishment. The act of administering shock is set in the context of a learning experiment, ostensibly designed to study the effect of punishment on memory. Aside from the experimenter, one naive subject and one accomplice perform in each session. On arrival each subject is paid $4.50. After a general talk by the experimenter, telling how little scientists know about the effects of punishment on memory, subjects are informed that one member of the pair will serve as teacher and one as a learner. A rigged drawing is held so that the naive subject is always the teacher, and the accomplice becomes the learner. The learner is taken to an adjacent room and strapped into an "electric chair".
>
> The naive subject is told that it is his task to teach the learner a list of paired associates, to test him on the list, and to administer punishment whenever the learner errs in the test. Punishment takes the form of electric shock, delivered to the learner by means of a shock generator controlled by the naive subject. The teacher is instructed to increase the intensity of electric shock one step on the generator on each error. The learner, according to plan, provides

many wrong answers, so that before long the naive subject must give him the strongest shock on the generator. Increases in the shock level are met by increasingly insistent demands from the learner that the experiment be stopped because of the growing discomfort to him (the deception is that the "learner", in fact, receives no shocks at all). The responses of the victim are standardised on tape, and each protest is co-ordinated to a particular voltage level on the shock generator. Starting with 75 volts the learner begins to grunt and moan. At 150 volts he demands to be let out of the experiment. At 180 volts he cries out that he can no longer stand the pain. At 300 volts he refuses to provide any more answers to the memory test, insisting that he is no longer a participant in the experiment and must be freed. In response to his last tactic, the experimenter instructs the naive subject to treat the absence of an answer as equivalent to a wrong answer, and to follow the usual shock procedure [1965, pp. 59–60].

One of the most striking results of this experiment is that over sixty percent of subjects continued to administer the shocks obediently until instructed to stop by the experimenter, even though they believed their actions were causing considerable pain to another person. During the experiment many of these subjects become anxious and concerned for the learner, but nevertheless continued to obey. There was a debriefing session following the experiment where the subjects were reassured that they had caused no harm to anyone.

Now in this experiment, the question is "Who would benefit from critical reflection on their experience?" From the subjects' point of view, they were debriefed—but the debriefing is hardly what one would call "critical reflection." They were told that everything was OK, that no one was hurt, and they should not feel bad because many other decent citizens continued to obey the experimenter's instructions—ignoring the point that they were easily duped by the unethical connivance of the experimenter! If the subjects were given the opportunity to reflect in a critical way on their experiences, perhaps following Brookfield's procedure, they would probably talk about their views of authority, the role of authority figures in their lives, the notion of personal responsibility, the assumption of trust they put in the experimenter, and ultimately the betrayal of this trust by the experimenter who deceived them. This was not part of the experiment. The reported reflection was that of the experimenter, and was wholly directed outward. He reflected on the psychological explanations for the subjects' obedience, using the language of social psychology: conformity, group norms, and so forth. At no stage did the experimenter critically reflect on his own action in conducting the experiment. If he had done so successfully, he might well have come to the view that his own part in the experiment was analogous to the part played by his subjects. What authority is he obeying in conducting an experiment based on deceit and subterfuge, which clearly creates anxiety and even anguish among the subjects? Just like the subjects he is studying, he continues right to the end—in the name of science. It is easy to see how such a conclusion escaped the experimenter, who was unable to step outside his own world. His conceptual machinery was applied to explaining the other but not the self.

This example illustrates (albeit in a hypothetical way) what is meant by critical reflection leading to assumptions being more inclusive and integrative of experience. If the experimenter had critically reflected on his own experience, and the result was as described, then he would have certainly had a more "inclusive and integrative" view of his experience. In Mezirow's terms, a perspective transformation would probably have occurred. But, as Mezirow points out, inclusiveness and integration cannot be the sole criteria for judging whether a perspective transformation results from critical reflection.

It is possible to have a "more inclusive and integrative" world view that actually distorts reality. For example, with conversion to a religious cult, it is common for the convert to reinterpret all prior experiences in a way that makes sense of the conversion, so that previous sins are now seen as a necessary part of the path to enlight-

enment. Thus a disjuncture in the convert's biography is reinterpreted as being part of a harmonious whole, which is more inclusive
and integrative of present experience. It is for this reason that it is
necessary to insist on further criteria for the success of critical reflection and perspective transformation. We must insist that the new
perspective remain open to alternative perspectives (see Mezirow),
and that it serves the interests of freedom rather than oppression.

Conclusion

The interpretation of experience is a social and political, as well
as a psychological exercise. The self as a fixed, stable, and harmonious entity is replaced by the notion of self-construction as an
ongoing process. The self in effect stands in a dialectical relationship to experience, both forming and being formed by the experience it encounters.

Chapter Eight

Establishing an "Adult" Teacher-Learner Relationship

The adult education literature has placed a great deal of emphasis on the importance of establishing an appropriate "adult" teacher-learner relationship. Because teachers and learners are adult peers, there is a widely held view that the relationship between teachers and adult learners should be participative and democratic and characterized by openness, mutual respect, and equality. To be sure, a relationship like this is desirable in all levels of education, but the political and social position of children presents a constraint that is not apparent in the adult context. Adults who are learners in one context may become teachers in another. In many instances, teachers of adults are the subordinates of their learners in the larger organizational or professional context. This role flexibility (and even ambiguity) in adult teaching and learning is not a feature of school-based education. But we should not be too complacent, as an ideal adult teacher-learner relationship is not something that emerges naturally from an adult teaching and learning situation. Issues of dominance, dependency, and control are as urgent in adult education as they are in school-based education.

What is the ideal adult teacher-learner relationship? As a first step in approaching this question, it is useful to distinguish three of its dimensions: the political, the philosophical, and the psychological. The political dimension has to do with how power should be distributed between the teacher and the learners and among learners. Who should determine when, where, how, and what will be learned? What special status and privileges, if any, should be accorded the teacher? Whose interests are served by a particular kind of teacher-learner relationship? There is thus a tension between the power of the teacher and the power of the learners. The philosophical dimension centers on how the relationship serves the purpose and aims of the educational activity. Does a particular aim or purpose, however derived, imply a certain kind of relationship? Does the curriculum constrain the nature of the relationship? The tension here is between traditional pedagogical demands associated with a given discipline and the requirements of an adult relationship. The psychological dimension is concerned with the attitudes, expectations, and actions of teachers and learners toward each other. The principal tension here is between the expectations and perceptions of learners and the expectations and perceptions of the teacher. In what follows, we are concerned with the political and psychological dimensions.

The Political Dimension

Freire's writings typify a primary concern with the politics of the teacher-learner relationship. In "liberating" or "problem-posing" education, he writes, "the teacher-of-the-students and the students-of-the-teacher cease to exist and a new term emerges: teacher-student with students-teachers. The teacher is no longer merely the one who teaches, but one who is himself taught in dialogue with the students, who in turn while being taught also teach. They become jointly responsible for a process in which all grow" (1972, p. 53). Interestingly enough, similar sentiments were expressed earlier this century by one of the founding fathers of liberal adult education, Mansbridge, who, in a 1913 publication entitled "University Tutorial Classes," maintained that the teacher of adults should be "in real fact a fellow student, and the fellow students are teachers" (Alfred, 1987).

These views are contrasted with their opposite, which Freire refers to as the "banking" concept of education, asserting that it mirrors oppressive society as a whole. Raul Anorve, a community educator who works with Mexican groups in Southern California, summarized Freire's distinction between the "banking" approach and the "problem-posing" approach in his address "Literacy for Empowerment" at the 1992 annual conference of the American Association of Adult Education.

In the banking approach

- The teacher determines the goals.
- The teacher is knowledgeable and the students are ignorant.
- The teacher imparts knowledge and skill and the students receive it.
- The teacher talks and the students listen.
- The students store the knowledge and skills for future use.
- The teacher directs the class sessions and the students comply.
- The education process perpetuates the status quo.

By contrast, in the problem-posing approach:

- The learners determine the goals.
- The facilitator and learners all have useful knowledge and skills.
- The learners soon apply the knowledge and skills in the pursuit of their goals.
- The facilitator and learners discuss issues.
- The facilitator and learners jointly decide the direction of class sessions.
- The education process helps create new realities.

Freire developed his ideas in the context of educating illiterate peasants in Brazil in the 1960s. Anorve used a Freirian approach in his work with Mexican migrants in the 1980s and the 1990s. They both have in common the desire to release the potential of education as a means by which domination and oppression can be thwarted. Myles Horton, working independently in the Highlander Folk School in Tennessee, advocated a similar approach in his work with labor unions in the 1930s and 1940s and in the civil rights movement of the 1950s and 1960s. He writes, "We realized it was necessary to learn how to learn from these people, so we started with the practical, with the things that were, and we moved from there to test our theories and our ways of thinking . . . we learned we had to take what people perceive their problems to be, not what we perceive their problems to be. We had to learn how to find out about the people, and then take that and put it into a program" (Horton, Kohl, and Kohl, 1990, p. 140).

At Highlander, everyone sits around in a circle to symbolize equality among all participants. Over the years more and more rocking chairs were introduced, so that now all chairs in the circle are rocking chairs, which seems to add to the poignancy of the learning-circle idea. Horton was concerned with education and follow-up action, as means or fostering a more democratic society, and so naturally he was concerned with distributing power among the learners. This should not be taken to mean that the teacher is neutral, far from it: "We also claimed no neutrality in presenting facts and ideas. What we sought was to set people's thinking apparatus in motion, while at the same time trying to teach and practice brotherhood and democracy" (1990, p. 152).

It is clear that power should be distributed evenly in community education, especially where there are strong common bonds and collective desire to act to bring about social justice. But are there lessons to be learned for those of us who work outside this context? Can power be distributed evenly where there are institutional constraints linked to accreditation practices and accountability to funding authorities, or where the students are pursuing individual rather than common goals?

Power and leadership are not necessarily the same. Although he was a committed community educator, Myles Horton did in fact exercise strong leadership and was very purposeful in pursuing his agenda. At the same time, it is important to recognize that community education, especially when it has a strong social justice agenda and a social action perspective, is really quite incompatible with practices in formal, bureaucratic educational institutions. Educators who work in these institutions still need to be aware of the potential for education to be either domesticating or liberating for those engaged in the process. Certainly silence, anxiety, fear, and powerlessness all interfere with learning and should be resisted on educational grounds alone. But how much power can realistically be distributed to students in organizational settings where the learning is certificated and the curriculum largely determined in advance? I pose this question because the political and psychological dimensions of the teacher-learner relationship are not really separable. Any institutionalized demarcation of power relationships will have consequences for the psychological relationship between teachers and learners. For example, trainers in industry are often seen as representing the interests of management rather than workers. They are often looked upon by management as essential to the implementation of new policies and organizational initiatives. When these policies and initiatives are perceived as being against the interests of workers, it is not possible to establish an ideal teacher-learner relationship.

The Psychological Dimension

Of course, there are many competing views about education as a political process and the nature and purpose of adult education. Whatever one's political or philosophical position, however, one can develop the teacher-learner relationship only in face-to-face encounters with learners. In an attempt to understand this dimension, adult education has borrowed from humanistic clinical psychology a set of concepts, terms, and practices aimed at facilitating the learner's self-awareness, growth, and self-esteem (see Rogers, 1983; Knowles, 1984). Not surprisingly, these practices are derived from clinical therapeutic techniques. This is evident in Rogers's concept of "facilitation," where he emphasizes the relationship between client (learner) and therapist (teacher). Rogers writes: "We know . . . [that] learning rests not upon the teaching skills of the leader, not upon scholarly knowledge of the field, not upon curricular planning, not upon use of audiovisual aids, not upon the programmed learning used, not upon lectures and presentations, not upon an abundance of books, though each of these might one time or another be utilized as an important resource. No, the facilitation of significant learning rests upon certain attitudinal qualities that exist in the personal relationship between the facilitator and the learner" (1983, p. 121).

He proceeds to identify the three core qualities of the good facilitator, which we summarize here:

1. Genuineness in entering into personal relationships with learners, rather than consistent adherence to the prescribed role of the teacher

2. Acceptance and trust in the learner as a person of worth (a quality similar to Rogers's "unconditional positive regard" toward the client)

3. Empathy (nonjudgmental understanding, both intellectual and emotional) for the learner's perspective

This emphasis on the personal relationship between the facilitator and the learner is also reflected in Knowles's views about establishing a climate for learning. He identifies a number of characteristics of a healthy psychological climate:

1. People are more open to learning when they are respected.

2. It is important for participants to be placed in a sharing relationship at the outset.

3. People learn more from those they trust than from those they mistrust, so it is important to establish a climate of mutual trust.

4. People learn better when they feel supported rather than judged or threatened.

5. A climate of openness and authenticity is also essential. When people feel free to be open and natural, to say what they really think and feel, they are more likely to be willing to examine new ideas [1990, pp. 127–128].

Too often, however, the humanistic view leads writers to propound sets of precepts that promise, if followed, to guarantee a smooth and harmonious relationship with learners. However, perfect harmony is rarely if ever found. Most adult education situations are full of potential sources of conflict, which, if unrecognized or misunderstood, can undermine the best efforts to establish an adult teaching environment. One source of conflict has to do with discrepancies between the teacher's conception of his or her role and the expectations of learners.

Salzberger-Wittenberg, Henry, and Osborne (1983) provide a good analysis of the dynamic interplay of conflicting teacher-learner expectations, aspirations, demands, projections, and fears. Working from a psychoanalytic base, they claim that many of the anxieties expressed by adult learners have their roots in childhood and infancy. In this way, adult expectations for education are associated with childhood feelings, especially toward parents and teachers. In extreme forms, they represent hopes or fantasies that can never be fulfilled. The following paragraphs describe four of these destructive expectations:

1. *The teacher is an ultimate source of knowledge and wisdom.* It is natural for learners to expect teachers to have more knowledge about their subject than they actually possess. However, learners often demand too much of teachers—they are generally not aware of the boundaries of teachers' expertise, and this is often exacerbated by staffing problems that require teachers to conduct classes outside their areas of expertise. In its extreme form, the expectation may be for a teacher who is nothing short of omniscient: "The wish for an all knowing teacher stems from the childhood feelings that the parents are the possessors of all knowledge and wisdom. The insistence on the imparting of information as the primary or (even)

exclusive object of education rests on the assumption that the adult knows all there is to be known and that this concrete bundle of knowledge can be taken over by the student as a package. Such a belief leads to the demand that the adult hand 'it' over, 'it' being a body of knowledge, an answer, a skill, a 'cure', or a perfect understanding" (p. 25).

2. *The teacher must be a provider and comforter.* As learners, we expect guidance and support from teachers, and we expect them to be willing to help. This expectation, taken to the extreme, can take the form of a demand that the teacher should be an automatic provider of all the student's needs and wishes. "Teachers, like others in the helping professions . . . easily become objects of infantile hopes: someone who will magically cure pain, take away frustration, helplessness, despair, and instead provide happiness and the fulfillment of all desires. . . . What is so dangerous in this attitude, and our tendency to fit in with it, is that it is anti-development, for as long as there is a persistent belief that the individual does not have to struggle with some frustration and mental pain he is not likely to discover or develop any latent strengths" (p. 28).

3. *The teacher is an object of admiration and envy.* It is natural for learners to admire the skill and knowledge of teachers—after all, it is something to which they are aspiring themselves. Salzberger-Wittenberg and the others argue that there is no admiration without some degree of envy. However, "when envy is uppermost, a person attacks and tries to destroy, in a variety of ways, the very thing he envies. . . . An envious person is likely to be good at finding out the teacher's weak points and playing on them. He may indeed succeed in undermining the teacher's confidence, make him feel depleted, be distracted, or, where envy is powerfully in operation, even unable to think" (p. 29).

4. *The teacher is a judge and authority figure.* Learners expect their work to be judged by the teacher—but often the exercise of this judgment leads to distress and hostility among learners, especially when it is seen as praise or blame. Also, learners attribute considerable power to teachers, and tend to be sure that teachers have

more institutional power than they actually possess. Once again, when teachers are viewed as failing to exercise their power in the learners' interests, or, worse still, as exercising it against their interests, resentment will result.

When teachers fail to live up to the learners' expectations (however unreasonable or excessive), the disappointment of learners will find expression—usually in the form of hostility toward the teacher and perhaps toward group members. The teacher too will have a set of expectations, fears, and aspirations that, when frustrated, may lead to behavior antithetical to an adult teaching-learning relationship (for example, hostile or infantile reactions to constructive criticism).

A similar analysis is offered by Williams (1993), who views the humanistic approach as being essentially "feminine" in character, especially with its emphasis on feelings, caring, and nurturance. In this view, humanistic adult educators—regardless of their gender—are positioned as feminine; the teacher in the humanistic classroom is in many ways analogous to the mother in the family:

> I use the analogy of the patriarchal family to illustrate the sorts of dynamics that can be generated from a culturally constructed set of gendered power relations and role expectations. Continuing the analogy, the question of the part the institution plays in this dynamic arises. In the family triad "dad" is, of course, the ultimate authority, the institution itself. Feminist and humanist teachers often experience split loyalties as does "mum" in trying to attend to the needs of both the child/student and father/institution. . . . When teachers side with the institution/father against the student/child, in order to protect their own interests, the student/child cannot help but feel betrayed. In such circumstances the student's anger and hostility toward the teacher is quite understandable [1993, pp. 57–58].

Williams also points out that the demand on the teacher to provide a safe and comfortable environment for learning is ultimately incompatible with the aim of extending and challenging students' beliefs, assumptions, and knowledge.

Whether or not one subscribes to these theoretical positions they have drawn attention to the need to make sense of the emotionality of adult teaching and learning, both from the learner's and teacher's point of view. One of the authors has developed a class exercise designed to highlight this aspect of adult teaching and learning (Tennant, 1991c). Adult educators who were enrolled in a formal course in adult education or were participating in a professional development seminar have taken part in this exercise over a period of several years. It requires participants to complete the tasks described below.

1. Identify aspects of student/trainee/participant behavior that annoy or irritate you. Provide specific examples if possible.
2. Identify aspects of your role which you fear and/or feel guilty about. Once again, provide specific examples if possible.

These tasks were designed with a number of considerations in mind. First, they attempt to gain indirect and implicit access to the participants' views of the adult teacher-learner relationship. Indirect access is essential, because requests for explicit statements on the nature of this relationship typically produce an ideal vision, which is useful for some purposes but which offers little insight into how teachers and learners work together in practice. Second, they focus on the feelings of the participants—their fears, guilt feelings, and annoyances. This stems from a belief that the emotional (and in this sense psychological) dimension of teaching and learning is at least as important a consideration as the political or philosophical dimensions. The tasks frankly focus on negative feelings because, while harmony and consensus are as much a feature of adult teaching and learning as conflict, conflict brings issues to the surface more quickly and sharpens tensions to the point where they are easily identified. In this instance, the goal is to understand some elements of the psychological conflicts apparent in adult

teaching and learning. By identifying their own fears, guilt feelings, and annoyances, the participants are indirectly indicating
how they perceive their role and responsibilities as adult educators. For example, if a teacher reports being annoyed by students'
failure to pay attention, then this indicates an underlying assumption that students have an obligation to pay attention at all times,
which may warrant some discussion.

Typical responses obtained in this exercise are documented in
Table 8.1.

Quite clearly, the demands that these adult educators impose
upon their learners are similar to what one would expect to find in
school-based education. Even though the language used to express
these demands is not overly authoritarian—there is no mention of
disobedience, delinquent behavior, and punitive action—the idea
that learners must participate, and on certain terms, is strongly present. Moreover, they are expected to have a certain generosity of
spirit toward the teacher, channeling any dissatisfaction into constructive criticism instead of hostile rejection. These responses were
obtained from experienced adult educators (both male and female)
who work in a variety of adult education settings: as trainers in
industry, commerce, or government departments; as community
workers, health educators, and basic educators; and as teachers of
English as a second language. The table should not be read as indicating any type of consensus. Rather, it shows the range of responses only, and there was considerable disagreement about
individual items.

This exercise is a way to focus on the way participants see their
role and responsibilities as adult educators. In the first stage of the
review process, participants discuss and analyze the annoyances they
listed, addressing questions such as "Why do you get annoyed at
that?" "Do you show your annoyance?" "In what circumstances
should you intervene?" "How can you intervene?" "What can you
do to avoid situations such as that?" Invariably, the discussion begins
to evoke basic questions about who sets the terms of participation,
the content and the process, and what is the purpose or motive of

Table 8.1. Teachers of Adults: Annoyances, Fears,
and Feelings of Guilt.

Annoyances with students	Fears	Guilt Feelings
1. Failure to participate. Examples: • Arriving late • Leaving early • Repeated absences • Not carrying out set tasks or activities • Indifference/apathy/ lack of involvement	1. Inability to meet needs because of lack of support from the system or weaknesses as a teacher.	1. Failure to meet needs. Examples: • Not being able to make contact with all members of the group • Not keeping a promise to the group • Presenting information one knows to be of little worth • Not being aware of what students want or need • Being overly influenced by vocal students
2. Violating the "terms" of participation. Examples: • Side conversations • Dominating comments • Racist/sexist comments • Impatience with slower learners • Not respecting the rights of others • Activities not related to the session such as sleeping or reading the newspaper	2. Inadequate expertise or knowledge. Examples: • Not being able to answer questions • Not fully understanding the subject matter	2. Lack of preparation. Examples: • Knowing what needs to be done but not doing it (applies to the full gamut of things a teacher can do to prepare for a session)

Table 8.1. Teachers of Adults: Annoyances, Fears, and Feelings of Guilt, Cont'd.

Annoyances with students	Fears	Guilt Feelings
3. Rejection of the content or process. Examples: • Statements about "knowing it all" • Criticisms of other learners • Explicit challenging of teacher's credentials and credibility • Refusal to consider new ideas or to listen to others' views • Personality characteristics of some learners, such as arrogance, antisocial behavior, ingratiating behavior, and competitiveness	3. Poor teaching and organizational skills. Examples: • Inability to hold interest • Losing one's place, getting confused, going blank • Not being able to complete the session • Failure of the technology • Inappropriate guest speakers	3. Inability to manage relationships of authority and control. Examples: • Exercising too much control or domination • Losing control of the group • Losing control of oneself, becoming angry or irritated

the group. The participants explore new ways of conceiving the adult teacher-learner relationship and analyze their implications. What is important here is that adult educators should be aware of the implicit assumptions and expectations contained in their attitudes toward learners' behavior. Exploring these assumptions helps them develop a clear conception of their role as teachers.

The concepts of *fear* and *guilt* are linked. What is a fear before the event will be transformed into a feeling of guilt after the event, especially where there is a perception of oneself as an agent. Fear of not being able to meet needs and guilt at not meeting needs were recurring features of these protocols. Perhaps it is because the idea of meeting needs is such an article of faith in adult education practice, and the reason that many engage in teaching adults in the first place. Associated with this is a fear of not having sufficient knowledge or expertise (what Brookfield [1990] refers to as the "impostor syndrome") and a fear of being inadequate as a teacher. The guilt connected with these two fears is expressed as centering on lack of preparation (this is what most people felt guilty about) and on the inability to manage authority relationships in the group. There was a strong concern about being too controlling and too dominant, but at the same time there was concern about losing control, and not preparing sufficiently to give strong guidance. There were large individual differences in what people referred to as control or dominance and as meeting needs, but they were present as issues in all the protocols. There was a strong sense in which these adult educators desired to retain certain teaching prerogatives and take on the responsibility for the success or quality of the course. But at the same time they were trying to decenter from the traditional training role and disperse authority, control, and decision making among the learners. This is perhaps the core dilemma for the adult educator, to maintain one's identity as a teacher and at the same time submerge this identity in the interests of the learners. Such a balancing act would be difficult on its own, even without the pressure of the usual adult education environment, where there are almost always competing claims about the respective roles of teachers and learners.

The interaction of the political and psychological dimensions of the teacher-learner relationship and the influence of relationships among the learners are illustrated in the following case study.

Case Study: Conflict in a Youth-Worker Training Course

The following is an account of tensions that arose in a course whose eighteen participants were employed in a housing assistance program for homeless youth. The course was divided into two five-day blocks. There were ten male and eight female participants. Nine of them lived in rural areas; they were accommodated during the course in a hotel near the training venue, and were therefore referred to as residential participants. The remaining participants commuted each day to the training venue. A conflict emerged during the first week of the course between some of the residential participants. The conflict centered around gender attitudes and behavior. During this first week there were two trainers working as a team, a principal trainer (male) and a co-trainer (female). The account of the incident is provided by the principal trainer.

> As the course progressed, some of the female members (and one in particular) clearly expected me to challenge every gender-based assumption or opinion voiced, regardless of its significance, context or its relevance to the session's content. This participant several times approached me privately to express disappointment that I had not done so. On the other hand, several male participants, including both the "key protagonists" and others, expected me (perhaps as a male), to challenge more often, and more strongly, the more assertive feminist statements by the female protagonists, again regardless of the significance, context or relevance to the session's content.
>
> Interestingly the men did not make these expectations known openly. I was acutely aware of them, but only through monitoring of participation levels in different activities non-verbal responses, interpretation of feedback invited after particular discussions, gossip, and accidental overhearing of conversations amongst participants.
>
> Among the residential group there were two women who worked together in an accommodation service for sexually abused young women. Both of these participants disclosed quite freely that they had been abused as children. There were also three males who overtly held very strong, I would say stereotypical, "traditional" male values. To return to the beginning, during the first two days of the course, my co-coordinator and I became aware that there was an uneasy tension in the group. We were aware of the spectrum of political values represented in the group, and suspected that a gender-based conflict was at play, but could see no evidence of its source. We noticed for example that the normal social interactions in such

groups were not developing at the pace we expected, that some participants were reluctant to work in small groups with some others, that participation in open discussions was guarded and subdued.

Despite special efforts to reinforce participation, activities to encourage "team spirit", and gentle introductions to "risk taking" and creative thinking etc, this defensive atmosphere persisted although no-one discussed its cause openly. At the start of the third morning, the tension in the training room was tangible.

During a discussion of alternative models of social services, and access to them, one of the female "protagonists" referred to the dominance of male doctors in the childbirth industry and advocated a greater role for women health professionals. A male "protagonist" responded sharply that men were involved in procreation as well, and the other female protagonist referred to him quite audibly as a "dickhead". An argument ensued.

It quickly emerged that the source of the group's tensions was behaviour by male "protagonists" outside the training environment (at meals and in the hotel) which was offensive to the female protagonists, and reaction by them which the males viewed as excessive, aggressive and "man-hating".

All attention in the group was obviously now focused on the conflict, which had nothing to do with the planned session content, and which had now totally usurped the learning process. Our immediate response was to re-assert the boundaries of group behaviour (disallowing personal attacks, allowing all viewpoints as legitimate input to discussions), quickly return to and finish dealing with the content under discussion, and announce an early tea break to be followed by de-briefing and discussion of the conflict incident [Yacopetti, 1993].

This account illustrates a number of issues relating to the teacher-learner relationship. First, there is the issue of the responsibilities and obligations of the coordinator to press ahead with the course content. This course was sponsored by an external client and the course content had been advertised prior to enrollment. The coordinator clearly feels obligated to cover the content, but recognizes that the conflict needs to be addressed. Early attempts to address the conflict, such as the use of activities to encourage team spirit, were obviously inappropriate. Such activities are typically employed to smooth over conflict rather than to address it in any fundamental way. The coordinator's desire to bring the conflict within his ambit of control, to make it a part of the workshop process, is also apparent in his naming of the subsequent discussion a debriefing, which is standard group process vernacular for winding up a planned exercise, as if the conflict had been engineered. Perhaps this was because the coordinators were aware that only five of the participants were centrally involved in the conflict (two women and three men) and that the remaining participants, although supporting one or the other of the protagonists' positions, were more concerned with the content of the course. A second issue concerns the role or posture of the coordinators. Should they attempt to be impartial or neutral? Or should they clearly express and enforce their views? The coordinator writes: "We clearly sympathized with the values of the women involved, and wished to reinforce and empower them in their advocacy of women's rights and challenge of sexist assumptions. On the other hand, we espouse a philosophy about learning in which we see the role of trainers as being neutral towards participants. That is, to be there for all participants, not just for those for whose values we agree. Yet again, to pretend to address the issue impartially, without judgment, would be inconsistent with our personal values" (Yacopetti, 1993, pp. 6–7).

The issue here is whether there are circumstances in which teachers should use their power and authority to effectively censor the views of participants. The difficulty of using this approach was that all the participants worked in the highly politicized field of youth homelessness, where gender issues are central. The coordinators had no choice but to address the conflict as the most pressing concern of the workshop.

Given the dynamics of the group, how can such conflict be addressed most effectively? The coordinators used the authority of their positions to set behavioral boundaries, disallowing personal attacks. They regained the initiative by setting aside a time for group discussion of the conflict. They split the group into two smaller groups to discuss the conflict, and then the two groups re-formed in an open forum. The result was reported as satisfactory, but there was a sense in which the issues were not really addressed: "participants were now avoiding any serious exploration of potentially contentious issues." The coordinators developed further strategies, such as shifting the focus of the discussion of gender issues to the workplace in general: "This allowed participants to generalise concepts and principles in a context which did not involve confrontation within the group, but did lead to reflection on the issues behind the group's conflict." This strategy had the effect of depersonalizing the conflict, separating the political issues from the psychological dynamics within the group. This final strategy is reported to have worked quite well in the sense that the protagonists finished the course on civil terms and several participants regarded the experience as valuable: "While not all members were fully satisfied at the end, the potentially destructive effect of the conflict was contained and managed." Once again, the emphasis is on containment rather than resolution. This is really the only possible solution, given the coordinators' view that they are there for all members of the group.

There are instances, however, where such neutrality is untenable, and this is arguably one of those instances. It is simply not possible to represent the interests of two groups whose interests clearly clash. Remaining neutral represents the interests of neither group, and the best that can be hoped for is a temporary neutralizing of the conflict. Another option is to pose the question "Whose interests am I prepared to defend?" It is the answer to this question that, ideally, should guide practice.

Conclusion

The foregoing discussion attempts to illustrate the various ways in which teaching is a site where the exploration of self and the struggle for power are both evident. In such an environment, it is vital that teachers of adults have a clear conception of their role. That is, that they have a posture as a teacher, and that they articulate this posture to the learners in a way that addresses their concerns and expectations. This is not to say that the posture should be inflexible and closed to negotiation and change. Rather, that neutrality and total malleability as a teacher (that is, not having a posture or stance) is not in the interests of developing an adult teacher-learner relationship. To adopt the role of a neutral facilitator of the group is to have a nonposture. In effect, it means that the identity of the teacher is out of focus, and is subject to the vagaries and whims of the learning group as it struggles to define its identity. At the other extreme, a rigid and nonnegotiable posture is equally damaging to the adult teacher-learner relationship. Some teachers vacillate between these two extremes, searching for a posture and identity that seems to work, some middle ground or compromise between violating and meeting conflicting expectations and needs. This is why teaching and learning are so emotionally charged—the whole interaction touches on our perception of self and how we relate to others. Moreover, it is a dynamic rather than static process, and contradiction and ambiguity are its driving forces. This being the case, the posture one develops as a teacher needs to be dynamic rather than static. That is, teachers need to acknowledge the inevitability and desirability of change and construct their approach to the job with a built-in conception of its own transformation. Without an awareness of what kinds of events or circumstances warrant a reconsideration of one's posture—and what do not—the ability to establish an adult teacher-learner relationship may be undermined by the conflicting demands and expectations imposed upon, and by, the learning group.

Chapter Nine

Teaching for Life-Span Development

Although most education is not consciously and explicitly directed toward psychological development, the process of education itself implies growth and development. Also, there is a considerable investment of the self in education. Even in highly technical or skills-based courses, the learner is concerned with questions that impact on the self. Students wonder, will I be able to perform at the level of proficiency required? Will I learn as quickly as the others? Will the teacher help me with the problems I may encounter? Do I have the background experience and knowledge to progress in this course? Will this course help achieve my goals in life? Will I relate well to the other students and will I be included in their social activities? Education is certainly a site which engages and challenges the self and which provokes self-reflection.

What does it mean then, to have a developmental perspective on teaching? First and foremost it means that as a teacher, you need to acknowledge and explore your own development and the place of teaching in your sense of self. Why were you drawn to teaching? What is the source of the satisfaction you derive from teaching? Do you have ambivalent attitudes to your role as a teacher? How do others see the role of teaching in your life? How do your current life concerns impact on your teaching? Has your teaching improved with experience? If so, in what ways? Have you changed your view about your role as a teacher and the purpose of your teaching? Do you act as a mentor for other teachers? How have you developed your knowledge and expertise in the domain in which you teach? Do you feel constrained in what you teach? If so, what is the source

191

of this constraint? The important thing is to pose questions such as these about your own teaching continually, so that your identity as a teacher is continually revisited and reconstructed.

The second aspect of having a developmental approach to teaching is to have a view about what development means, both within the confines of the domain in which you teach, and more broadly. This will enable you to understand and respond to learners' developmental needs and to challenge and promote developmental progress in the broadest way possible.

The Development of Teaching Expertise

Brookfield (1990) offers some advice on how to become a skillful teacher. The advice includes "be clear about the purpose of your teaching . . . reflect on your own learning . . . be wary of standardized models and approaches . . . expect ambiguity . . . [and] recognize the emotionality" of learning. In a final note he remarks, "Don't trust what you have just read"! This is reminiscent of Groucho Marx saying he would never join a club that would have him as a member, or the old paradox where a citizen of Crete says "All Cretans are liars." Brookfield's final advice may evoke amusement or even offense, but his advice should be taken seriously. He is pointing to the paradoxical, ambiguous, and even contradictory nature of teaching practice. He goes on to explain: "What for me are truths of skillful teaching may, for you, be partially or entirely inappropriate. Keep in mind that in the time between writing this manuscript and its publication I may have amended some of these truths, deleted others, and added still more. My continuing journey as a teacher through diverse contexts and dilemmas is bound to generate new insights" (1990, p. 210). Brookfield is discounting the possibility that one can talk of teaching expertise devoid of context and without some reference to the ongoing development of teaching expertise. What he is saying with respect to the influence of context is consistent with the notion of expertise and autonomy discussed in earlier chapters: that they are context and domain-specific. "What is effective in one context, with one student or group of students, or for one purpose may be severely dysfunctional in another context, with different people, or for another purpose" (1990, pp. 192–193).

This ability to read and adjust to the context in which one is working certainly appears to be a developmental phenomenon. Shulman (1987) also highlights this quality as being a characteristic of the skillful teacher. He recounts the case of Nancy, a twenty-five-year veteran English teacher who was observed on two occasions. On the first occasion, "She was like a symphony conductor, posing questions, probing for alternative views, drawing out the shy while tempering the boisterous. Not much happened in the classroom that did not pass through Nancy, whose pacing and ordering, structuring and expanding, controlled the rhythm of classroom life" (p. 2). On the second occasion, when she was sick and unable to talk because of laryngitis, she was observed using small group techniques with reporting back from each group. Although the style had changed radically, the outcome was similar; the students were engaged and the subject matter was treated with care. Shulman notes, "Thus Nancy's pattern of instruction, her style of teaching, is not uniform or predictable in some simple sense. She flexibly responds to the difficulty and character of the subject matter, the capacities of the students and her educational purposes" (p. 3).

That Nancy is able to respond in a flexible way to the demands of the context shows that she has at her disposal a range of teaching techniques and methods. While this is a necessary condition for being a skillful teacher, it is by no means sufficient. It is also necessary to be able to read the context and select an appropriate response—an ability embedded in what Shulman refers to as the "wisdom of practice," which is consistently cited as a feature of higher levels of expertise and development. Shulman is right to call for a more sustained research effort to document this wisdom of practice: to collect, collate, and interpret the practical knowledge of teachers and how this knowledge is developed.

Brookfield also refers to the value-laden nature of determining what constitutes effective teaching.

> Effectiveness is also irredeemably value laden. The decision concerning effectiveness rests on certain judgments and interpretations. Whenever one concept of effectiveness gains ascendancy over others, the power struggles between groups that are seeking to define this concept in their own ways are clearly evident. What are effective behaviours for one group of teachers may be examples of psychological bludgeoning for another. What one teacher may consider an effective teaching effort a student may see as a demeaning experience. So talking about effectiveness as if it were an objective concept whose features can be easily agreed on by all reasonable people is mistaken. We always have to ask, Effective for what? and Effective for whom? [1990, p. 193].

By extension, this same observation can be applied to views about what constitutes the development of teaching expertise. Indeed, as we have argued, what constitutes development generally is subject to value judgments. Thus the development of expertise cannot be an isolated exercise—development can only make sense through a community of others who share a common value system. What constitutes development generally, or development in any particular area of expertise, is contested—different groups have different interests in what passes as development. This really cannot be otherwise. What it means is that development is always tentative in that it is always within a framework of commonly shared assumptions and beliefs. What is important is that these assumptions and beliefs be public and open to scrutiny, so that one's development as a teacher is always open to revision and reframing.

The Meaning of Development

What we have tried to show in the preceding pages is that it is simply not possible to construct an abstract and universal model of development that transcends questions of value, which are ultimately political questions.

The view of development advocated here has a number of features, as described below.

Development Is Multidimensional

It has always been possible to point to different types of development, such as the development of intelligence, cognition, social roles, moral understanding, identity, and so on. But even within these different developmental domains there are now a host of dimensions previously unrecognized. For example, in Chapters One and Two, we illustrated how conventional views of intelligence and cognition have been challenged in recent years. The early murmuring about the cross-cultural validity of intelligence tests opened up options for reconceptualizing intelligence. If intelligence can only be understood within a particular cultural context, then it needs to include context as one of its defining features. What about adulthood as a context? Do existing measures of intelligence really capture what it means to be an intelligent person in working, family, and community life? The answer appeared to be No! The notion of crystallized intelligence was an early attempt to capture the nature of adult intelligence. This was followed by the more recent idea of the pragmatics of intelligence. Chapter Three introduced a more radical departure from the intelligence-testing tradition, with the concept of practical intelligence and the development of expertise, wisdom, and tacit knowledge during adult life. Thus the history of the concept of intelligence records increasing recognition of the diverse ways in which people can express their intelligence: in formal tests, in problem solving, in making judgments, and in practical engagement with the world.

In Chapters Four and Five, we saw how there have always been different approaches to documenting the development of the self. But these different approaches are essentially competing theories— they are rival claims to the truth about development, so to speak.

Although each recognizes diversity, this diversity is contained within an overall framework of development tailored to its own world view. Chapter Five illustrated how culture and history play a role in shaping both the theoretical and popular frameworks through which we see development. This is clearly apparent even within Western culture, where theories of development have been contested as being dominated by male perspectives. Once again, it is not possible to talk about development outside of its cultural and historical context.

Does the idea of "development in context" lead into a morass? How can the teacher avoid the rather nihilistic nonposition of relativism? What use is the theoretical literature if it is all relative? We believe that it is certainly useful to have an understanding of the theoretical literature, and that the problem of relativism can be addressed. First, it is worth repeating and expanding Collins's point (1991) about the relation between theory and practice: "It is more efficacious to think in terms of engaging thoughtfully with theory and, then, putting *ourselves* in to practice. In other words, serious engagement with theoretical models improves our potential as reflective practitioners" (p. 47).

Thus theory does not provide a foundation of knowledge that is then applied to practice in the ordinary sense. Instead, it is used as a base for reflection on practice. Weathersby (1981) expresses the use of such theory in the following way:

> It can . . . heighten our appreciation of shared patterns of differences among students. If we tune our ears so that we can hear students across different frameworks of meaning, we are more likely to communicate effectively and to respond with an appropriate form of support or challenge. Familiarity with the patterns of ego development can create simple and profound difference in our perceptions, attitudes, and behavior as we approach teaching. . . . We are more likely to listen to students' frames of references, to ask for their reasons and feelings about a situation, to expect patterns of diversity, and to value responses that represent advances in development regardless of our norms of expected levels of achievement [p. 72].

Thus theory represents part of the ongoing dialogue that informs adult education practice. But a second point needs to be made: the theoretical literature can help educators form considered views about what constitutes development. It is not sufficient to take the relativistic position that anything can pass for development, nor the overly eclectic view, applying one theory to one situation and another theory to a different situation. The working view should be based on formal theory, expanded and tempered by practice and observation of the teacher's own classes. Whatever view of development you espouse, we argue that it should take into account the context in which you work, and that you should be able to articulate and justify the values and assumptions that underpin the view.

There Are Multiple Developmental Pathways

The foregoing chapters imply that in whatever domain one chooses, or whatever goals are formulated, development can and will take different routes. The nature, timing and processes of development will vary according to the experiences and opportunities of individuals and the circumstances of their lives. What this means for teaching, in the first instance, is that one should not have a singular conception of the proper or most efficient route to development. For example, if you want learners to develop autonomy in the subject matter you teach, you need to have a view about the path that best promotes autonomy. This will probably include some idea of your role in introducing and providing a framework for understanding the core concepts or basic skills needed for autonomy. You will probably turn to your own experience—how did you develop a sense of autonomy in this subject matter? However, it is a mistake to assume that your pathway is the best guide to others' pathways. Turning to experience is fine, but it needs to be done in a critical way. A little reflection may reveal that these basic skills can be acquired in other ways, or that they turn out not to be basic skills at all. What is required here is a certain amount of openness to experimentation and other possibilities. This general attitude of openness is in fact a frequently cited attribute of those who successfully develop expertise in their work.

Notwithstanding the above, some common processes that trigger development can be identified among the various theories. These include

1. Encouraging students to attend to and reflect on experience
2. Having peer groups work together on common issues or problems with opportunity for the exchange of ideas
3. Exposing students to situations that create ambiguity or conflict when existing frameworks for understanding are shown to be inadequate—with support for resolving the conflict
4. Recognizing student achievements
5. Placing students in situations requiring new responses and actions
6. Providing students relative freedom from internal and external constraints and anxiety, and encouraging them to explore and take risks

Many of these processes are consistent with current views about what constitutes good adult education practice (see Hayes, 1993, for a review of current perspectives on teaching adults). At the same time, they are all problematic and require interpretation, elaboration, and extension.

Development Is Both Individual and Social

The idea of development has meaning only in terms of a cultural and historical framework. In the foregoing chapters, we have argued that development is essentially a dialectical process. The raw materials in the process of development are the organism, with its constitutionally endowed equipment; and the social environment, with its historically given social and cultural formations. Development thus proceeds through a constant interaction between the person and the social environment. Both the developing person and the social environment are active in this process. This is why it is referred to as dialectical. However, it is easy to see that the social-environment side of this dialectical relationship is the more powerful. For the developing person, the social environment appears as a fact, a product of nature with truths that need to be discovered. Through everyday social interactions (peer/peer, parent/child, child/school, adult/work), the social world becomes not only regulative of the person, but a part of personal identity. There are opportunities to resist social molding, and many developmental theories point to such resistance as a hallmark of development: "developed" individuals are represented as becoming more autonomous or as transcending conventional social rules and regulations. In the adult education literature, the source of resistance is the person's capacity to critically reflect, with others, on his or her social and cultural assumptions. But, as writers like Usher point out, even when one understands the nature of one's social and cultural world, it retains its force. Another way of seeing resistance is to understand one's experience as a text and to explore alternative readings of this text. This is precisely the approach adopted in gender, race, and class struggles for social justice. Such struggles provide alternative readings to texts of the lives of those who have suffered oppression: readings that reinterpret history and personal biographies and thereby legitimize and support alternative identities.

Because development is contested, and because different versions of development serve the interests of different groups, it is as much a political as it is a psychological construct. Teachers need to understand how the group can be used both to oppress and to liberate, and how alternative readings of learners' biographies can be constructed to make sense of their demands and actions. Teaching for development thus implies an understanding of race, gender, and class conflict.

Conclusion

It is important to avoid a static conception of development. In a given life history, identity is constantly changing and open to reconstruction. Personal changes stem from historical changes in the surrounding culture and also from the individual life cycle. A person's age-related social category changes over the years, bringing a whole complex of changed expectations from others. Quite apart from these sources of developmental change, there is always the possibility of constructing a new identity, based on a better understanding of one's biography and greater self-awareness. Education is one of a number of experiences that can trigger this sort of growth, as well as other more conventional kinds of change. But education for development is not restricted to promoting fundamental changes in the worldview of learners. It can also promote other, more conventional kinds of change through assisting learners to adjust to socially expected developmental tasks. What is important, however, is that these developmental tasks be approached in a critical way, with an understanding of how social and cultural origins serve the interests of different groups in society. Ultimately, adult educators need to distinguish between education that simply domesticates learners and education that is genuinely developmental.

References

Alexander, C. N., and Langer, E. J. *Higher Stages of Human Development.* Oxford, England: Oxford University Press, 1990.

Alfred, D. "Albert Mansbridge." In P. Jarvis (ed.), *Twentieth Century Thinkers in Adult Education.* London: Croom Helm, 1987.

Anderson, J. R., and Kosslyn, S. M. (eds.). *Tutorials in Memory and Learning Essays in Honor of Gordon Bower.* San Francisco: Freeman, 1984.

Andresen, L. "Teaching University Teachers to Teach—While They Teach." A *Quarterly Experience*, 1991, 26, 14–17.

Anorve, R. "Literacy for Empowerment." Paper presented at the annual conference of the American Association of Adult and Continuing Education, Los Angeles, Nov. 1992.

Archard, D. *Children: Rights and Childhood.* London: Routledge, 1993.

Ariès, P. *Centuries of Childhood.* London: Penguin, 1962.

Arin-Krupp, J. "Over 40? Here's to Growth." Paper presented at the 39th Annual Conference of the American Association of Adult and Continuing Education, Salt Lake City, Utah, Oct. 31–Nov. 2, 1990.

Arlin, P. K. "Cognitive Development in Adulthood: A Fifth Stage?" *Developmental Psychology*, 1975, 11, 602–606.

Arlin, P. K. "Adolescent and Adult Thought: A Structural Interpretation." In M. L. Commons, F. A. Richards, and C. Armon (eds.), *Beyond Formal Operations: Late Adolescent and Adult Cognitive Development.* New York: Praeger, 1984.

Arlin, P. K. "Problem Finding and Young Adult Cognition." In R. A. Mines and K. S. Kitchener (eds.), *Adult Cognitive Development: Models and Methods.* New York: Praeger, 1986.

Arlin, P. K. "Wisdom: the Art of Problem Finding." In R. J. Sternberg (ed.). *Wisdom: Its Nature, Origins, and Development.* Cambridge, England: Cambridge University Press, 1990.

Baltes, P. B. "Longitudinal and Cross-Sectional Sequences in the Study of Age and Generation Effects." *Human Development*, 1968, 11, 145–171.

Baltes, P. B. "Theoretical Propositions of Lifespan Developmental Psychology:

On the Dynamics Between Growth and Decline." *Developmental Psychology*, 1987, 23(5), 611–626.

Baltes, P. B., and Willis, S. L. "Plasticity and Enhancement of Intellectual Functioning in Old Age: Penn State's Adult Development and Enrichment Project (ADEPT)." In F.I.M. Craik and S. E. Trehub (eds.), *Aging and Cognitive Processes*, New York: Plenum, 1982.

Baltes, P. B., Cornelius, S., and Nesselroade, J. "Cohort Effects in Developmental Psychology." In J. Nesselroade and P. B. Baltes (eds.), *Longitudinal Research in the Study of Behavior and Development*. New York: Academic Press, 1980.

Baltes, P. B., Dittman-Kohli, F., and Dixon, R. A. "New Perspectives on the Development of Intelligence in Adulthood: Toward a Dual-Process Conception and a Model of Selective Optimization with Compensation." In P. B. Baltes and O. G. Brim, Jr. (eds.), *Life-Span Development and Behavior*. Vol. 6. New York: Academic Press, 1984.

Baltes, P. B., Reese, H., and Lipsitt, L. "Lifespan Developmental Psychology." *Annual Review of Psychology*, 1980, 31, 65–110.

Basseches, M. "Dialectical Schemata: A Framework for the Empirical Study of Dialectical Thinking." *Human Development*, 1980, 23, 400–421.

Basseches, M. *Dialectical Thinking and Adult Development*. Norwood, N.J.: Ablex Publishing, 1984.

Benack, S. "Postformal Epistemologies and the Growth of Empathy." In M. L. Commons, F. A. Richards, and C. Armon (eds.), *Beyond Formal Operations: Late Adolescent and Adult Development*. New York: Praeger, 1984.

Boud, D. "Experience as Base for Learning." *Higher Research and Development*, 1992, 12(1), 33–44.

Boud, D., and Walker, D. "Making the Most of Experience." *Studies in Continuing Education*, 1990, 12(2), 61–80.

Boud, D., and Walker, D. *Experience and Learning: Reflection at Work*. Geelong, Australia: Deakin University Press, 1991.

Boud, D., and Walker, D. "In the Midst of Experience: Developing a Model to Aid Learners and Facilitators." In J. Mulligan and C. Griffin (eds.), *Empowerment through Experiential Learning*. London: Kogan Page, 1992.

Boud, D., Keogh, R., and Walker, D. (eds.). *Reflection: Turning Experience into Learning*. London: Kogan Page, 1985a.

Boud, D., Keogh, R., and Walker, D. "What is Reflection in Learning?" In D. Boud, R. Keogh, and D. Walker (eds.), *Reflection: Turning Experience into Learning*. London: Kogan Page, 1985b.

Brookfield, S. "Self-Directed Learning: a Conceptual and Methodological Exploration." *Studies in the Education of Adults*, 1985, 17(1), 19–32.

Brookfield, S. *Developing Critical Thinkers*. San Francisco: Jossey-Bass, 1987.

Brookfield, S. *The Skillful Teacher*. San Francisco: Jossey-Bass, 1990.

Brookfield, S. "Using Critical Incidents to Explore Assumptions." In J. Mezirow and Associates, *Fostering Critical Reflection in Adulthood*. San Francisco: Jossey-Bass, 1991.

Brookfield, S. "Self-Directed Learning, Political Clarity, and the Critical Practice of Adult Education." *Adult Education Quarterly*, 1993, 43(4), 227–242.

Broudy, H. S. "Tacit Knowing and Aesthetic Education." In R. S. Smith (ed.), *Aesthetic Concepts and Education*. Urbana: University of Illinois Press, 1970.

Bruner, J. *Beyond the Information Given*. New York: Norton, 1973.

Buss, A. R. "Dialectics, History, and Development: The Historical Roots of the Individual-Society Dialectic." In P. B. Baltes and O. G. Brim, (eds.), *Life-span Development and Behavior*. New York: Academic Press, 1979.

Caffarella, R., and Olson, S. "Psychosocial Development of Women." *Adult Education Quarterly*, 1993, 43(3), 125–151.

Candy, P. C. *Self-Direction for Lifelong Learning*. San Francisco: Jossey-Bass, 1991.

Carraher, T. N., Carraher, D. W., and Schliemann, A. D. "Mathematics in the Streets and in the Schools." *British Journal of Developmental Psychology*, 1985, 3, 21–29.

Cattell, R. B. *Abilities: Their Structure, Growth, and Action*. Champaign, Ill.: IPAT, 1971.

Ceci, S. J., and Bronfenbrenner, U. " 'Don't Forget to take the Cupcakes out of the Oven': Prospective Memory, Strategic Time-Monitoring, and Context." *Child Development*, 1985, 56, 175–190.

Ceci, S., and Liker, J. "Academic and Non-Academic Intelligence: an Experimental Separation." In R. J. Sternberg and R. Wagner (eds.), *Practical Intelligence: Nature and Origins of Competence*. Cambridge, England: Cambridge University Press, 1986.

Chase, W., and Simon, H. "Perception in Chess." *Cognitive Psychology*, 1973, 4, 55–81.

Chi, M.T.H. "Knowledge Structures and Memory Development." In R. Siegler (ed.), *Children's Thinking: What Develops?* Hillsdale, N.J.: Erlbaum, 1978.

Chi, M.T.H., Glaser, R., and Farr, M. J. (eds.). *The Nature of Expertise*. Hillsdale, N.J.: Erlbaum, 1988.

Chickering, A. W., and Havighurst, R. "The Life Cycle." In A. W. Chickering (ed.), *The Modern American College*. San Francisco: Jossey-Bass, 1981.

Cole, M., Gay, J., Glick, J. A., and Sharp, D. W. *The Cultural Context of Learning and Thinking*. New York: Basic Books, 1971.

Collins, M. *Adult Education as Vocation: A Critical Role for the Adult Educator*. London: Routledge, 1991.

Courtenay, B. "Are Psychological Models of Adult Development Still Important for the Practice of Adult Education?" *Adult Education Quarterly*, 1994, 44, 145–153.

Crittenden, B. "Autonomy as an Aim of Education." In K. O. Strike and K. Egan (eds.), *Ethics and Educational Policy*. London: Routledge & Kegan Paul, 1978.

Cross, K. P. *Adults as Learners*. San Francisco: Jossey-Bass, 1981.

Datan, N., and Lohmann, N. (eds.). *Transitions of Aging*. New York: Academic Press, 1980.

Davies, B. *Frogs and Snails and Feminist Tales*. Sydney, Australia: Allen & Unwin, 1989.

De Corte, E. "Towards Powerful Learning Environments for the Acquisition of Problem Solving Skills." *European Journal of Psychology of Education*, 1990, 5, 5–19.

De Groot, A. D. "Perception and Memory Versus Thought: Some Old Ideas and Recent Findings." In B. Kleinmuntz (ed.), *Problem Solving*. New York: Wiley, 1966.

de Mause, L. (ed). *The History of Childhood*. New York: Psychohistory Press, 1976.

Denney, N. W. "Problem Solving in Later Adulthood: Intervention Research." In P. B. Baltes and O. G. Brim, (eds.), *Life-span Development and Behavior*. Vol. 2. New York: Academic Press, 1979.

Deshler, D. "Metaphor Analysis: Exorcising Social Ghosts." In J. Mezirow (ed). *Fostering Critical Reflection in Adulthood*. San Francisco: Jossey-Bass, 1991.

Dewey, J. *Experience and Education*. New York: Collier, 1963.

Dittman-Kohli, P. "Towards a Neofunctionalist Conception of Adult Intellectual Development: Wisdom as a Proto-typical Case of Intellectual Growth." In A. Langer, *Beyond Formal Operations: Alternative Endpoints to Human Development*. New York: Cambridge University Press, 1985.

Dittman-Kohli, F., and Baltes, P. B. "Toward a Neofunctionalist Conception of Adult Intellectual Development: Wisdom as a Proto-typical Case of Intellectual Growth." In C. Alexander and E. Langer (eds.), *Beyond Formal Operations: Alternative Endpoints to Human Development*. New York: Oxford University Press, 1986.

Dixon, R. A., and Baltes, P. B. "Toward Lifespan Research on the Functions and Pragmatics of Intelligence." In R. J Sternberg and R. K. Wagner (eds.), *Practical Intelligence: Nature and Origins of Competence*. Cambridge, England: Cambridge University Press, 1986.

Dube, E. F. "Literacy, Cultural Familiarity and 'Intelligence' as Determinants of Story Recall." In U. Neisser (ed.), *Memory Observed: Remembering in Natural Contexts*. San Francisco: W. H. Freeman, 1982.

Ehrlich, K., and Soloway, E. "An Empirical Investigation of the Tacit Plan Knowledge in Programming." In J. C. Thomas and M. L. Schneider (eds.), *Human Factors in Computer Systems*. Norwood, N.J.: Ablex, 1979.

Eisner, E. (ed.). *Learning and Teaching the Ways of Knowing*. Chicago: University of Chicago Press, 1985.

Eraut, M. "Knowledge Creation and Knowledge Use in Professional Contexts." *Studies in Higher Education*, 1985, 10(2), 117–133.

Erikson, E. H. "Identity and the Life Cycle." *Psychological Issues*, 1959, 1, 1 (Monograph No. 1).

Evans, G., and Butler, J. "Expert Models and Feedback Processes in Developing Competence in Industrial Trade Areas." *Training Research Conducted in*

Higher Education. Conference/Workshop sponsored by the National Center for Vocational Research, Ltd. Sydney, Australia: July 1992.

Evans, N. "Pragmatism at Work in Britain: Some Reflections on Attempting to Introduce Assessment of Prior Experiential Learning." *Studies in Continuing Education*, 1990, 12, 2, 122–130.

Evans, N. "Linking Personal Learning and Public Recognition." In J. Mulligan and C. Griffin (eds.), *Empowerment through Experiential Learning*. London: Kogan Page, 1992.

Findler, N. V. (ed.). *Associative Networks: Representation and Use of Knowledge by Computers*. New York: Academic Press, 1979.

Ford, M. E. "Social Cognition and Social Competence in Adolescence." *Developmental Psychology*, 1982, 18(3), 323–340.

Ford, M. E. "For All Practical Purposes: Criteria for Defining and Evaluating Practical Intelligence." In R. J. Sternberg and R. Wagner (eds.), *Practical Intelligence: Nature and Origins of Competence in the Everyday World*. Cambridge, England: Cambridge University Press, 1986.

Foucault, M. "Technologies of the Self." In L. Martin, H. Gutman, and P. Hutton (eds.), *Technologies of the Self*. London: Tavistock, 1988.

Freire, P. *Pedagogy of the Oppressed*. Harmonsworth: Penguin, 1972.

Freire, P. *Education: The Practice of Freedom*. London: Writers and Readers, 1974.

Gardner, H. *Frames of Mind*. New York: Basic Books, 1985a.

Gardner, H. *The Mind's New Science*. New York: Basic Books, 1985b.

Gentner, D. R. "Expertise in Typewriting." In M. Chi, R. Glaser, and M. Farr, (eds.), *The Nature of Expertise*. Hillsdale, N.J.: Erlbaum, 1988.

Ghisselli, E. *The Validity of Occupational Aptitude Tests*. New York: Wiley, 1966.

Gibb, J. R. "Learning Theory in Adult Education." In M. S. Knowles (ed.), *Handbook of Adult Education in the United States*. Washington, D.C.: American Association of Adult and Continuing Education, 1960.

Gibbs, B. "Autonomy and Authority in Education." *Journal of Philosophy of Education*, 1979, 13, 119–132.

Gilligan, C. *In a Different Voice*. Cambridge, Mass.: Harvard University Press, 1986.

Gladwin, T. *East Is a Big Bird*. Cambridge, Mass.: Harvard University Press, 1970.

Glaser, R. *The Nature of Expertise*. (Occasional Paper No. 107.) Columbus, Ohio: National Center for Research in Vocational Education, 1985.

Glaser, R. "Thoughts on Expertise." In C. Schooler and K. W. Schaie (eds.), *Cognitive Functioning and Social Structure over the Life Course*. Norwood, N.J.: Ablex, 1987.

Goodnow, J. J. "Some Lifelong Everyday Forms of Intelligent Behavior: Organizing and Reorganizing." In R. J. Sternberg and R. K. Wagner (eds.), *Practical Intelligence: Nature and Origins of Competence*. Cambridge, England: Cambridge University Press, 1986.

Gould, R. *Transformations: Growth and Change in Adult Life*. New York: Simon & Schuster, 1978.

Gould, R. "The Therapeutic Learning Program." In J. Mezirow (ed.), *Fostering Critical Reflection in Adulthood*. San Francisco: Jossey-Bass, 1990.

Griffin, C. *Curriculum Theory in Adult and Lifelong Education*. London: Croom Helm, 1983.

Griffin, C. *Adult Education and Social Policy*. London: Croom Helm, 1987.

Gutmann, D. *Reclaimed Powers: Toward a New Psychology of Men and Women in Later Life*. New York: Basic Books, 1987.

Hager, P., and Gonczi, A. "Attributes and Competence." *Australian and New Zealand Journal of Vocational Educational Research*, 1993, 1(1), 36–45.

Harrison, P. L., Kaufman, A. S., Hickman, J. A., and Kaufman, N. L. "A Survey of Tests Used for Adult Assessment." *Journal of Psychoeducational Assessment*, 1988, 6, 188–198.

Hart, M. U. "Liberation Through Consciousness Raising." In J. Mezirow (ed.), *Fostering Critical Reflection in Adulthood*. San Francisco: Jossey-Bass, 1990.

Havinghurst, R. J. *Developmental Tasks and Education*. (3rd ed.) New York: McKay, 1972.

Hayes, E. "Current Perspectives on Teaching Adults." *Adult Education Quarterly*, 1993, 43(93), 173–186.

Hooykaas, R. *Religion and the Rise of Modern Science*. Edinburgh: Scottish Academic Press, 1972.

Horn, J. L. "Organization of Data on Lifespan Development of Human Abilities." In L. R. Goulet and P. B. Baltes (eds.), *Lifespan Developmental Psychology: Research and Theory*. New York: Academic Press, 1970.

Horn, J. L. "The Aging of Human Abilities." In B. B. Wolman (ed.), *Handbook of Developmental Psychology*. Englewood Cliffs, N.J.: Prentice-Hall, 1982.

Horowitz, L. L. "Head and Hand in Education: Vocationalism Versus Professionalism." *School Review*, 1975, 83, 397–414.

Horton, M., Kohl, J., and Kohl, H. *The Long Haul: An Autobiography*. New York: Doubleday, 1990.

Houle, C. O. *The Literature of Adult Education: A Bibliographic Essay*. San Francisco: Jossey-Bass, 1992.

Howard, D. V. "Implicit and Explicit Assessment of Cognitive Aging." In M. L. Howe and C. J. Brainerd (eds.), *Cognitive Development in Adulthood*. New York: Springer-Verlag, 1988.

Hoyer, W. J. "Aging and the Development of Expert Cognition." In T. M. Schlecter and M. P. Toglia (eds.), *New Directions in Cognitive Science*. Norwood, N.J.: Ablex., 1985.

Hyde, J., and Phillips, D. "Androgyny Across the Lifespan." *Developmental Psychology*, 1979, 15, 334–336.

Ikels, C. "Becoming a Human Being in Theory and Practice: Chinese Views of Human Development." In D. I. Kertzer and K. W. Schaie (eds.), *Age Structuring in Comparative Perspective*. Hillsdale, N.J.: Erlbaum, 1989.

Irwin, M. A. "Emic and Unfamiliar Category Sorting of Maro Farmers and U.S.

Undergraduates." Journal of Cross-Cultural Psychology, 1974, 4, 407–423.

Irwin, R. R. "Reconceptualizing the Nature of Dialectical Postformal Operational Thinking: The Effects of Affectively Mediated Social Experiences." In J. D. Sinnott and J. C. Cavanaugh (eds.), Bridging Paradigms: Positive Development In Adulthood and Cognitive Aging. New York: Praeger, 1991.

Jarvis, P. Adult Learning in the Social Context. London: Croom Helm, 1987a.

Jarvis, P. "Meaningful and Meaningless Experience: Toward an Analysis of Learning from Life." Adult Education Quarterly, 1987b, 37, 164–172.

Jarvis, P. Paradoxes of Learning. San Francisco: Jossey-Bass, 1992.

Kaufman, A. S. Assessing Adolescent and Adult Intelligence. Boston: Allyn and Bacon, 1990.

Kaufman, A. S., Reynolds, C. R., and McLean, J. E. "Age and WAIS-R Intelligence in a National Sample of Adults in the 20 to 74 Year Age Range: A Cross-Sectional Analysis with Education Level Controlled." Intelligence, 1989, 13, 235–254.

Kitchener, K., and King, P. "A Reflective Judgment Model: Transforming Assumptions about Knowing." In J. Mezirow (ed.), Fostering Critical Reflection in Adulthood. San Francisco: Jossey-Bass, 1991.

Kitchener, K., and King, P. Developing Reflective Judgment. San Francisco: Jossey-Bass, 1994.

Knowles, M. The Adult Learner: A Neglected Species. Houston, Tex.: Gulf Publishing, 1978.

Knowles, M. (ed.). Andragogy in Action. San Francisco: Jossey-Bass, 1984.

Knowles, M. "Fostering Competence in Self-Directed Learning." In R. M. Smith and Associates, Learning to Learn Across the Lifespan. San Francisco: Jossey-Bass, 1990.

Knox, A. "Programming for Adults Facing Mid-Life Change." New Directions for Continuing Education, 1979, 2, 1–135.

Knox, A. B. Strengthening Adult and Continuing Education: A Global Perspective on Synergistic Leadership. San Francisco: Jossey-Bass, 1993.

Kohlberg, L., and Ryncarz, R. A. "Beyond Justice Reasoning: Moral Development and Consideration of a Seventh Stage." In C. N. Alexander and E. J. Langer. (eds.), Higher Stages of Human Development. Oxford, England: Oxford University Press, 1990.

Kolb, D. Experiential Learning. Englewood Cliffs, N.J.: Prentice-Hall, 1984.

Kramer, D. A. "Post-Formal Operations: A Need for Further Conceptualization." Human Development, 1983, 26, 91–105.

Labouvie-Vief, G. "A Life-Span View of Social Cognition." Educational Gerontology, 1980a, 12(4), 277–290.

Labouvie-Vief, G. "Adaptive Dimensions of Adult Cognition." In N. Datan and N. Lohmann (eds.), Transitions of Aging. New York: Academic Press, 1980b.

Labouvie-Vief, G. "Beyond Formal Operations: Uses and Limits of Pure Logic in Lifespan Development." *Human Development,* 1980c, 23, 141–161.

Labouvie-Vief, G. "Intelligence and Cognition." In J. E. Birren and K. W. Schaie (eds.), *Handbook of the Psychology of Aging.* (2nd ed.) New York: Van Nostrand Reinhold, 1985.

Langer, E. J., and others. "Nonsequential Development and Aging." In C. N. Alexander and E. J. Langer (eds.), *Higher Stages of Human Development.* New York: Oxford University Press, 1990.

Lau, D. C. (trans.) *The Analects.* Bergenfield, N.J.: Penguin Books, 1979.

Lave, J. "Cognitive Consequences of Traditional Apprenticeship Training in West Africa." *Anthropology and Educational Quarterly,* 1977a, 8, 177–180.

Lave, J. "Tailor-made Experiments and Evaluating the Intellectual Consequences of Apprenticeship Training." *The Quarterly Journal of the Institute of Comparative Human Cognition,* 1977b, 2, 21–25.

Lawrence, J. "Expertise on the Bench: Modelling Magistrates' Judicial Decision-Making." In M.T.H. Chi, R. Glaser, and M. J. Farr (eds.), *The Nature of Expertise.* Hillsdale, N.J.: Erlbaum, 1988.

Lesgold, A. M. "Acquiring Expertise." In J. R. Anderson and S. M. Kosslyn (eds.), *Tutorials in Memory and Learning: Essays in Honor of Gordon Bower.* San Francisco: Freeman, 1984.

Levinson, D. *The Seasons of a Man's Life.* New York: Knopf, 1978.

Loevinger, J. *Ego Development.* San Francisco: Jossey-Bass, 1976.

Lukes, S. *Individualism.* Oxford, England: Basil Blackwell, 1973.

McClusky, H. "The Relevance of Psychology for Adult Education." In G. Jensen, A. A. Liverwright, and W. Hallenbeck (eds.), *Adult Education: Outlines of an Emerging Field of University Study.* Washington, D.C.: American Association of Adult and Continuing Education, 1964.

McCoy, V. "Adult Life Cycle Change: How Does Growth Affect Our Education Needs?" *Lifelong Learning: The Adult Years,* 1977, 31, 14–18.

Maslow, A. *Toward a Psychology of Being.* New York: Van Nostrand Reinhold, 1968.

Merriam, S., and Clark, M. *Lifelines: Patterns of Work, Love, and Learning in Adulthood.* San Francisco: Jossey-Bass, 1991.

Mezirow, J. *Fostering Critical Reflection in Adulthood: A Guide to Transformative and Emancipatory Learning.* San Francisco: Jossey-Bass, 1990.

Mezirow, J. *Transformative Dimensions of Adult Learning.* San Francisco: Jossey-Bass, 1991.

Miles, T. R. "Contributions to Intelligence Testing and the Theory of Intelligence." *British Journal of Educational Psychology,* 1957, 27, 153–165.

Milgram, S. "Some Conditions of Obedience and Disobedience to Authority." *Human Relations,* 1965, 18(1), 57–76.

Minois, G. *History of Old Age.* Chicago: University of Chicago Press, 1987.

Murtaugh, M. "The Practice of Arithmetic by American Grocery Shoppers." *Anthropology and Education Quarterly*, 1985, 16, 186–192.

Myles-Worsley, M., and Johnston, W. A. "The Influence of Expertise on X-Ray Image Processing." *Journal of Experimental Psychology, Learning, Memory, and Cognition*, 1988, 14(3), 553–557.

Neisser, U. "General, Academic and Artificial Intelligence." In L. B. Resnick (ed.), *The Nature of Intelligence*. Hillsdale, N.J.: Erlbaum, 1976.

Neisser, U. "The Concept of Intelligence." *Intelligence*, 1979, 3, 217–227.

Neugarten, B. "Adaptation and the Life Cycle." *Counselling Psychologist*, 1976, 6, 16–20.

Norman, D. A. *The Psychology of Everyday Things*. New York: Basic Books, 1988.

Partridge, Y. M. "Personal Autonomy and Compulsory Liberal Education." Unpublished doctoral dissertation, University of British Columbia, 1979.

Perkins, D. N., and Salomon, G. "Are Cognitive Skills Context-Bound?" *Educational Researcher*, 1989, 18, 16–25.

Perry, W. *Forms of Intellectual and Ethical Development in the College Years*. New York: Holt, Rinehart and Winston, 1968.

Peters, J. "The Action-Reason-Thematic Technique: Spying on the Self." In J. Mezirow and Associates, *Fostering Critical Reflection in Adulthood*. San Francisco: Jossey-Bass, 1991.

Piaget, J. "Intellectual Evolution from Adolescence to Adulthood." *Human Development*, 1972, 15, 1–12.

Piaget, J. *The Development of Thought: Equilibration of Cognitive Structures*. Oxford, England: Basil Blackwell, 1978.

Piaget, J., and Inhelder, B. *The Psychology of the Child*. New York: Basic Books, 1969.

Polanyi, M. *The Tacit Dimension*. London: Routledge and Kegan Paul, 1967.

Richards, F. A., and Commons, M. L. "Postformal Cognitive-Developmental Theory and Research: A Review of Its Current Status." In C. N. Alexander and E. J. Langer (eds.), *Higher Stages of Human Development*. New York: Oxford University Press, 1990.

Riegel, K. F. "Dialectical Operations: The Final Period of Cognitive Development." *Human Development*, 1973, 16, 346–370.

Riegel, K. F. "Adult Life Crises: A Dialectical Interpretation of Development." In N. Datan and L. H. Ginsberg (eds.) *Lifespan Developmental Psychology*. New York: Academic Press, 1975.

Riegel, K F. "The Dialectics of Human Development." *American Psychologist*, Oct. 1976, 689–699.

Riley, M. W. "On the Significance of Age in Sociology." *American Sociological Review*, 1987, 52(1), 1–14.

Rogers, C. *Client-Centered Therapy*. Boston: Houghton Mifflin, 1951.

Rogers, C. *Freedom to Learn for the 1980s*. Columbus, Ohio: Merrill, 1983.

Rogoff, B., and Lave, J. (eds.). *Everyday Cognition: Its Development in Social Context.* Cambridge, England: Cambridge University Press, 1984.

Rosenstock, L. "The Walls Come Tumbling Down: the Overdue Reunification of Vocational and Academic Education." *Phi Delta Kappan,* Feb. 1991.

Rybash, J., Hoyer, W., and Roodin, P. *Adult Cognition and Aging.* New York: Pergamon Press, 1986.

Säljö, R. "Learning about Learning." *Higher Education,* 1979, 8, 443–451.

Salzberger-Wittenberg, I., Henry, G., and Osborne, E. *The Emotional Experience of Learning and Teaching.* London: Routledge, 1983.

Sangree, W. H. "Age and Power: Life-Course Trajectories and Age Structuring of Power Relations in East and West Africa." In D. I. Kertzer and K. W. Schaie (eds.), *Age Structuring in Comparative Perspective.* Hillsdale, N.J.: Erlbaum, 1989.

Schaie, K. "A General Model for the Study of Developmental Problems," *Psychological Bulletin,* 1965, 64, 92–107.

Schaie, K. W. "Age Changes in Adult Intelligence." In D. Woodruff and J. Birren (eds.), *Aging: Scientific Perspectives and Social Issues.* New York: Van Nostrand, 1975.

Schaie, K. W. "The Seattle Longitudinal Study: A 21-year Exploration of Psychometric Intelligence in Adulthood." In K. W. Schaie (ed.), *Longitudinal Studies of Adult Psychological Development.* New York: Guildford Press, 1983.

Schaie, K. W., and Hertzog, C. "Fourteen-Year Cohort-Sequential Analyses of Adult Intellectual Development." *Developmental Psychology,* 1983, 19, 531-543.

Schaie, K. W., and Willis, S. "Can Adult Intellectual Decline be Reversed?" *Developmental Psychology,* 1986, 22, 223–232.

Schmidt, H. G., Norman, G. R., and Boshuizen, H.P.A. "A Cognitive Perspective on Medical Expertise: Theory and Implications." *Academic Medicine,* 1990, 65(10), 611–621.

Schön, D. A. *The Reflective Practitioner.* New York: Basic Books, 1983.

Schön, D. A. *Educating the Reflective Practitioner.* San Francisco: Jossey-Bass, 1987.

Scribner, S. "Cognitive Studies of Work." *The Quarterly Newsletter of the Laboratory of Comparative Human Cognition,* 1984a, 6, 1–2.

Scribner, S. "Studying Working Intelligence." In B. Rogoff and J. Lave, *Everyday Cognition: Its Development in Social Context.* Cambridge, Mass.: Harvard University Press, 1984b.

Scribner, S. "Thinking in Action: Some Characteristics of Practical Thought." In R. J. Sternberg and R. Wagner (eds.), *Practical Intelligence: Nature and Origins of Competence.* Cambridge, England: Cambridge University Press, 1986.

Scribner, S., and Cole, M. "Cognitive Consequences of Formal and Informal Education." *Science,* 1973, 182, 553–559.

Scribner, S., and Fahrmeier, E. "Practical and Theoretical Arithmetic: Some Preliminary Findings." *Report: Industrial Literacy Project,* 1982.

Senge, P. M. *The Fifth Dimension*. Sydney, Australia: Random House, 1990.

Shapin, S., and Barnes, B. "Head and Hand: Rhetorical Resources in British Pedagogical Writing, 1770–1850." *Oxford Review of Education*, 1976, 2(3), 231–254.

Shulman, L. "Knowledge and Teaching: Foundations of the New Reform." *Harvard Educational Review*, 1987, 57(1), 1–22.

Simosko, S. *APL: A Practical Guide for Professionals*. London: Kogan Page, 1991.

Sinnott, J. D. "Postformal Reasoning: The Relativistic Stage." In M. L. Commons, F. A. Richards, and C. Armon (eds.), *Beyond Formal Operations: Late Adolescent and Adult Cognitive Development*. New York: Praeger, 1984.

Smith, J. "Explorations of Wisdom and Positive Changes with Age." Paper presented at the 5th Australian Developmental Conference, Sydney, Aug. 26–28, 1988.

Smith, R. "Implementing the Learning to Learn Concept." In A. Tuijnman and M. van der Kamp, *Learning Across the Lifespan*. Elsmford, N.Y.: Pergamon Press, 1992.

Souvaine, E., Lahey, L. L., and Kegan, R. "Life after Formal Operations: Implications for a Psychology of the Self." In C. N. Alexander and E. J. Langer (eds.). *Higher Stages of Human Development: Perspectives on Adult Growth*. New York: Oxford University Press, 1990.

Spilich, G. J. "Text Processing of Domain Related Information for Individuals with High and Low Domain Knowledge." *Journal of Verbal Learning and Verbal Behavior*, 1979, 18, 275–290.

Sternberg, R. J. *Beyond IQ: A Triarchic Theory of Human Intelligence*. New York: Cambridge University Press, 1984a.

Sternberg, R. J. "Toward a Triarchic Theory of Human Intelligence." *The Behavioral and Brain Sciences*, 1984b, 7, 269–315.

Sternberg, R. J. "Intelligence." In R. J. Sternberg and E. E. Smith (eds.), *The Psychology of Human Thought*. Cambridge, England: Cambridge University Press, 1988a.

Sternberg, R. J. "Mental Self-Government: A Theory of Intellectual Styles and their Development." *Human Development*, 1988b, 31, 197–224.

Sternberg, R. J. (ed.). *Wisdom: Its Nature, Origins, and Development*. Cambridge, England: Cambridge University Press, 1990a.

Sternberg, R. J. "Intelligence and Adult Learning." Papers from an Institute Sponsored by the Center for Adult Learning Research, Montana State University, 1990b.

Sternberg, R. J., and Caruso, D. R. "Practical Modes of Knowing." In E. Eisner, (ed.), *Learning and Teaching the Ways of Knowing*. Chicago: University of Chicago Press, 1985.

Sternberg, R. J., and Wagner, R. K. (eds.). *Practical Intelligence: Nature and Origins of Competence in the Everyday World*. Cambridge, England: Cambridge University Press, 1986.

Streufert, S., and Streufert, S. C. *Behavior in the Complex Environment*. Washington, D.C.: Winston, 1978.

Tennant, M. *Psychology and Adult Learning*. London: Routledge, 1988.

Tennant, M., *Adult and Continuing Education in Australia*. London: Routledge, 1991a.

Tennant, M. "Establishing an Adult Teaching-Learning Relationship." *Australian Journal of Adult Education*, 1991b, 31(1), 4–9.

Tennant, M. "Expertise as a Dimension of Adult Development: Implications for Adult Education." *New Education*, 1991c, 13(1), 46–57.

Tennant, M. "Perspective Transformation and Adult Development." *Adult Education Quarterly*, 1993, *44*, 34–42.

Thomas, J. C., and Schneider, M. L. (eds.). *Human Factors in Computer Systems*. Norwood, N.J.: Ablex, 1979.

Usher, R. "Beyond the Anecdotal: Adult Learning and the Use of Experience." *Studies in the Education of Adults*, 1985, 17(1), 59–74.

Usher, R. "Adult Students and their Experience: Developing a Resource for Learning." *Studies in the Education of Adults*, 1986, 18(1), 24–34.

Usher, R. "Locating Experience in Language: Towards a Post Structuralist Theory of Experience." *Adult Education Quarterly*, 1989, 40(1) 23–32.

Usher, R. "Experience in Adult Education: a Post-Modern Critique." *Journal of Philosophy of Education*, 1992, 26, 201–214.

Usher, R. "Disciplining Adults: Re-examining the Place of Disciplines in Adult Education." *Studies in Continuing Education*, 1993, 15, 98–116.

Wagner, R. K., and Sternberg, R. J. "Tacit Knowledge and Intelligence in the Everyday World." In R. J. Sternberg and R. K. Wagner (eds.), *Practical Intelligence: Nature and Origins of Competence*. Cambridge, England: Cambridge University Press, 1986.

Walker, R. E., and Foley, J. M. "Social Intelligence: Its History and Measurement." *Psychological Reports*, 1973, 33, 839–864.

Walters, J. M., and Gardner, H. "The Theory of Multiple Intelligences: Some Issues and Answers." In R. J. Sternberg and R. K. Wagner (eds.), *Practical Intelligence: Nature and Origins of Competence*. Cambridge, England: Cambridge University Press, 1986.

Weathersby, R. "Ego Development." In A. W. Chickering (ed.), *The Modern American College*. San Francisco: Jossey-Bass, 1981.

Wei-Ming, T. "The Confucian Perception of Adulthood." In E. Erikson (ed.), *Adulthood*. New York: Norton, 1978.

Wigdor, A. K., and Garner, W. R. *Ability Tests: Uses, Consequences, and Controversies*. Washington, D. C.: National Academy Press, 1982.

Williams, C. "The Politics of Nurturant Teaching." *Studies in Continuing Education*, 1993, 15(1), 50–62.

Yacopetti, D. Unpublished manuscript. Sydney, Australia: University of Technology, Sydney, 1993.

Yourcenar, M. *Memoirs of Hadrian*. Harmondsworth: Penguin, 1959.

Zimbardo, P. *Psychology and Life*. (9th ed.) Glenview, Ill.: Scott, Foresman, 1976.

Index